ALSO BY DOTTY GRIFFITH

The Texas Holiday Cookbook

Cooking with Days of Our Lives

Gourmet Grains, Beans and Rice

Wild About Munchies

Wild About Chili

Dallas Cuisine

EDITED BY DOTTY GRIFFITH

The Mansion on Turtle Creek Cookbook
by Dean Fearing

SIMON & SCHUSTER
NEW YORK • LONDON • TORONTO • SYDNEY • SINGAPORE

DOTTY GRIFFITH

celebrating
barbecue

*the ultimate guide to america's
four regional styles of 'cue*

★

SIMON & SCHUSTER
Rockefeller Center
1230 Avenue of the Americas
New York, New York 10020

For information about special discounts for bulk purchases,
please contact Simon & Schuster Special Sales:
1-800-456-6798 or business@simonandschuster.com

Illustrations by Renée Herman
Book design and map by Kevin Hanek; set in Monotype Bulmer

Manufactured in the United States of America

1   2   3   4   5   6   7   8   9   10

Library of Congress Cataloging-in-Publication Data is available.

ISBN 978-1-4516-2764-0

acknowledgments

This book is dedicated to Kelly and Caitlin, my wonderful son and daughter.
Thanks for smelling, tasting, and eating so much barbecue.

Thanks also to the many friends I've made through writing about barbecue and judging
barbecue cook-offs over the past twenty-plus years. For encouragement
and help as sources and for guiding me to other sources, thanks to
Karen Adler, John T. Edge, Bob Garner, Hubert Green, Smoky Hale,
Michael LeMaster, Gary Puckett, Jim Tabb, and Carolyn Wells.
For tasting and testing recipes, thanks to Martha Hershey.
For research, thanks to Michele Axley.

As always, thanks to my agent, Dedie Leahy, for her faith and trust,
and to my editor, Sydny Miner, for her confidence in the idea.

contents

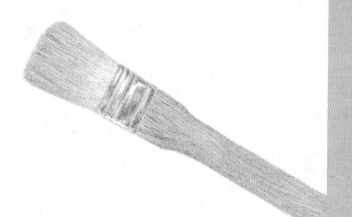

PART ONE ★

an invitation to die

Writing a book about barbecue is almost guaranteed to garner more death threats than dinner invitations. Few subjects incite more passion. Consequently, just about all the outdoor cooks who fire up a kettle grill on the patio think their brisket/ribs/pork recipe is pretty darn good, maybe even the best. And if that's what they think, they're right. I wouldn't argue . . . although I might make a suggestion.

It's been said that all politics is local. The same applies to barbecue. And barbecue is personal. Very personal. The barbecue that most of us love best is the kind we grew up with (if we're fortunate enough to come from a native barbecue region) or the style that first passed our lips. Barbecue imprints powerfully on the palate and the soul. One's first taste of barbecue is never the last, but that first taste leaves an impression that lasts a lifetime.

Barbecue is the most American of foods; to hell with apple pie. If Congress decided to declare a national dish, barbecue should win by acclamation. I can't think of anything else that generates as much anticipation, excitement, controversy, competition, and festivity. Yet it is a food born of deprivation, hard times, cheap ingredients, and simple equipment—very much like another American original, jazz. Often intertwined (especially in the regional styles of Memphis and Kansas City), barbecue and jazz are uniquely American and specifically Southern, yet appreciation of these art forms migrated east, north, west, and beyond the seas as well.

Like the roots of jazz, the basis of the cooking technique we call barbecue originates in the South, most likely in what became the state of North Carolina. While Americans and cooks all over the world have adapted barbecue basics to local preferences, four regional styles—Carolina, Memphis, Texas, and Kansas City—dominate and define the genre.

A point of clarification: This book is about barbecue—long, slow cooking over low temperatures—not grilling, which is fast cooking over high heat. Sometimes grilling is used to finish or glaze barbecue, but virtually everything in this book takes hours, not minutes. In general, to barbecue means to cook directly over or beside coals at a temperature of 212° to 300°F. Sometimes the temperature inside the cooker may go a bit higher. No problem as long as it comes back down. A bit lower? No problem if not for too long.

The target temperature is just above the boiling point, to heat the moisture in the meat without evaporating it. And that's cooking low and slow—i.e., barbecuing.

Within that rather narrow range of temperatures, a lot of different things can happen. Given the differences in styles of barbecue, it is amazing how similar the basic processes are. So what makes the difference?

THE FOUR GREAT STYLES OF AMERICAN BARBECUE

		CAROLINA	MEMPHIS	TEXAS	KANSAS CITY
MEAT		Pork, whole hog and shoulder	Pork, ribs and shoulder	Beef brisket, pork ribs	Pork ribs, beef brisket
RESULTS		Pulled and chopped pork; vinegar-based sauces, with and without tomato, or mustard based	Wet ribs (sticky, with lots of tomato-based sauce) and dry ribs (without sauce during cooking)	Sliced brisket with tomato-based sauce on the side; glazed ribs with tomato-based sauce on the side	Sticky ribs with lots of tomato-based sauce; sliced brisket with tomato-based sauce on the side
TECHNIQUES		Pit cooked, direct heat	Smoked over indirect heat; finished over direct heat	Smoked over indirect heat; finished over direct heat	Indirect heat; finished over direct heat
FLAVOR PROFILE		Hot-sour	Sweet, hot, smoky	Savory, smoky, touch of sweet	Sweet-sour, hot

The characteristics that distinguish regional barbecue styles—meat, fuel, sauce, and results—are remarkably consistent within regions and vary greatly from one region to another. In the Carolinas the meat is pork; the fuel is oak or hickory; the mandatory sauce is vinegar based; and the meat may be served as shredded or chopped pork sandwiches topped with coleslaw.

Pork is the meat of choice throughout the South. In Alabama, Georgia, Florida, and Mississippi the styles are basically mergers of the pure Carolina style, with redder, sweeter sauces, culminating in the pulled pork of Tennessee and Kentucky, where sauces are thicker. But the real signature of Southern barbecue is Memphis ribs.

Whether those ribs are served wet or dry is a bone of contention. The ribs are, of course, pork; the fuel is hickory or oak. The wet or dry issue relates to the sauce and whether it is brushed on the ribs (wet) during cooking or served on the side (dry).

In Texas the meat is beef; the signature fuel is mesquite; the optional sauce is tomato based and served at the table; and the meat is dramatically seasoned with peppery spice blends called rubs and may be served as thin-sliced brisket with sides like beans and potato salad.

Between those poles of style and geography lies Kansas City, the barbecue world's Constantinople, where East meets West and beef meets pork. The meat can be either beef brisket or pork ribs; the fuel is hickory or fruitwood; the sauce, usually sweet and hot, is as important as the meat; and the finished product is very tender, sticky with sauce. In Kansas City what you put the sauce on matters less than the sauce itself. The meat can be chicken, beef brisket, spare or baby back ribs, lamb, or anything else that takes to fire, smoke, and sauce.

None of this means that you can't find good examples outside their respective regions. In fact, you can find cooks practicing these styles—and hybrids—all over the United States. This is, after all, about barbecue, not culinary, regional, or ethnic purity.

BARBECUE REGIONS OF THE UNITED STATES

Because Kansas City–style sauce was the prototype for the nation's first bottled version, sauce is what defines *barbecue* for many. People who live farther from the barbecue heartland are more likely to think of barbecue as anything that comes off a grill with barbecue sauce on it.

Pork barbecue reigns throughout the Carolinas and the rest of the South, with sauce variations from vinegary to tomatoey.

In Memphis the rib becomes almighty, but pulled pork with a thick tomato sauce is a strong tradition as well.

Texas barbecued beef brisket rules in cattle country.

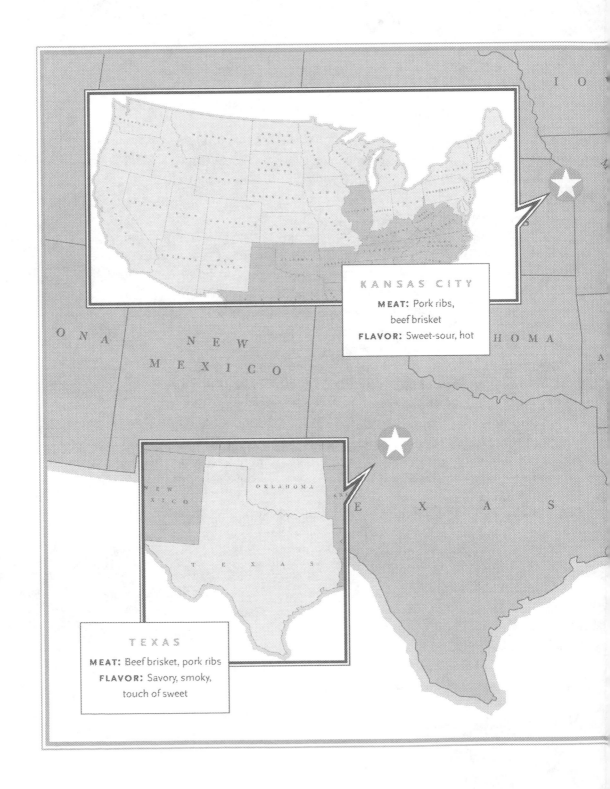

KANSAS CITY

MEAT: Pork ribs, beef brisket

FLAVOR: Sweet-sour, hot

TEXAS

MEAT: Beef brisket, pork ribs

FLAVOR: Savory, smoky, touch of sweet

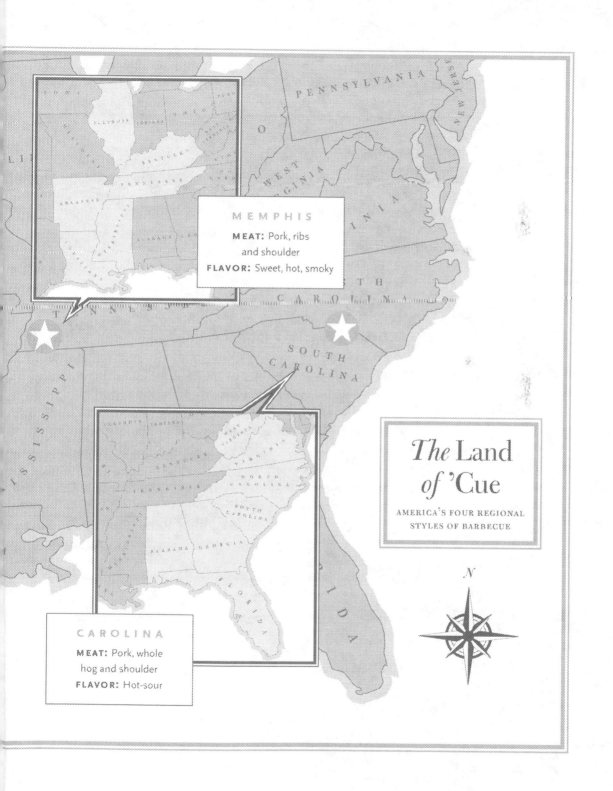

MEMPHIS
MEAT: Pork, ribs and shoulder
FLAVOR: Sweet, hot, smoky

CAROLINA
MEAT: Pork, whole hog and shoulder
FLAVOR: Hot-sour

The Land *of* 'Cue

AMERICA'S FOUR REGIONAL STYLES OF BARBECUE

N

"If you're born and raised on it [a certain style], that's what you like."
—Jim Tabb, barbecue judge and rub maker, Tryon, North Carolina

"Barbecue is low and slow; grilling is hot and fast."
—Carolyn Wells, Kansas City Barbecue Society, Kansas City, Missouri

"If it moves, we cook it."
—Carolyn Wells, Kansas City Barbecue Society, Kansas City, Missouri

"The best sauce is homemade because it's the freshest.
Use a bottled sauce only when time requires you to."
—Ardie Davis, *The Great Barbecue Sauce Book*

me and 'cue

Where I grew up in northeast Texas, beef brisket and barbecue are synonymous. Sausage, chicken, or ribs might be included on a combo plate or at a cookout. Hickory is the wood of choice around home. Geographically and spiritually, this part of the state is closer to the Deep South and the hardwood forests of Arkansas and Louisiana. Mesquite from the scrubby tree of the same name is the favorite wood in the southwestern parts of the state and has come to be an identifying characteristic of Texas barbecue, but Texans use a lot of oak as well.

For years I never thought much about the origin of barbecued ribs, which were, of course, pork. At that time, to me—and to hardcore Texas loyalists—barbecue was beef. The anomaly of pork ribs was a dirty little secret, but this mostly unacknowledged inconsistency foreshadowed a personal epiphany.

My first experiences with barbecue other than Texas style came through my travels, particularly as a food journalist. My first encounter with dry ribs at The Rendezvous in Memphis was as reassuring and familiar as pulled pork sandwiches with coleslaw were strange and exotic. Except that the place was so nice and the waiters so proper. That seldom happens in a Texas joint.

Hooked on the differences as well as the similarities, I was into barbecue diversity before diversity was cool.

Whether it is a blessing or a curse I don't know, but I love to try things I've never had before, so my ingrained barbecue bias has never been an impediment. A marker and a baseline maybe, but never a source of prejudice against other styles. I'll try damn near anything, which can be very helpful when it comes to barbecued "snoots." More about them later.

Although I'd read about Carolina-style barbecue, this Texan was still surprised years ago when I first encountered strings of shredded gray pork at the annual Memphis in May contest, where I was a judge in 1984. Wan and pale, the meat was seasoned with thin, vinegary sauces flecked with pepper that seemed to me more like marinades. But again, the reality of the succulent meat and the vibrant tang of the sauces shook my world. What a discovery! Especially the crisp bits of skin and fat chopped in to provide textural contrast to the satiny meat. So different and so wonderful for a barbecue virgin from Terrell, Texas.

Family ties as well as work took me to Kansas City many times over the years. Once again I encountered similarities to Texas barbecue, particularly in the beef brisket. After tasting Kansas City ribs, however, I should have clicked on the importance of sauce, but I failed to appreciate the locals' magnificent obsession until I met one of the 'cue queens of K.C., Karen Adler. She has done a lot to school me in the ways of barbecue, not only in Kansas City but elsewhere. Just how fascinated are Kansas Citians with barbecue sauce? They love to make it, collect it, and use it. A nephew from Kansas City, Charles Rhodes, now lives in

North Carolina, and he maintains two shelves of barbecue sauce in his pantry, mostly from Gates Barbecue, his hometown favorite. He never fails to bring some back when he goes home; friends and family bring him more when they visit. This young man has a Depression-era mentality, characteristic of his grandparents' generation, about barbecue sauce. He simply can't have too much on hand. Although still deeply committed to Kansas City barbecue, particularly brisket, this stalwart drove me from one end of North Carolina to the other tasting pork barbecue. If not converts, at least now we're educated.

Judging barbecue contests like Memphis in May and the Jack Daniel's Invitational has given me a chance to meet a lot of cooks and sauce freaks; to taste and see the various styles. What I've learned is that fascination with barbecue is as universal as the human fascination with fire.

After cooking my way through the recipes in this book, I've also come to the conclusion that pork, specifically pork shoulder, is the best meat for barbecue. It is the easiest to cook and the hardest to screw up. Brisket requires a lot of baby-sitting. With ribs, - you've got to have the right touch. A whole hog . . . well, that's a tough one for most of us even to contemplate. But shoulder—with a sweet, hot Kansas City sauce or a tangy Memphis-style sauce—*that's* the ultimate barbecue for the home cook and the best starter recipe I can recommend.

I know my Texas friends consider me blasphemous to endorse pork shoulder. But I've yet to cook a shoulder that didn't turn out just fine. And I've messed up a few briskets.

barbecue:
past, present, and future

THEN AND NOW

Researching barbecue is like herding cats. There are so many theories, so many sources, that it's hard to get the subject under control. For every rule there are fourteen exceptions. For every "thou shalt," there are six "thou shalt nots" . . . except when this happens or in case that happens.

That's really why I wrote this book. While trying to find out about regional barbecue styles for another writing project, I couldn't find a source that compared, contrasted, and attempted to codify the subject. Through further research and while writing, I discovered why there wasn't such a source. The subject defies codifying. Even harder than herding cats, reducing barbecue to a set of specifications is like teaching a cat to bark. The task contradicts the nature of the art form. Still, if art historians can do it for Impressionism, I'm willing to give it a try for barbecue.

I've used broad language to explain the styles, knowing full well that someone can—and probably will—find a nit to pick with almost every point. I fully expect, as this book makes its way through barbecue circles, to be told how much I still don't know about barbecue by devotees wanting to set the record straight. Fine—bring it on.

Lots of sources give bits and pieces about the various styles of barbecue, and of course, whole books have been devoted to the subject in general or to a region in particular. Still, there wasn't a body of work that put the major points of difference and similarity between two covers. So here goes, starting with the history of barbecue and the origin of the word.

There seems to be considerable agreement that barbecue as we know it began in North Carolina. An anonymous tract published in London around 1666 describes hogs, wild and domestic, as being so plentiful and easy to raise or catch that the colonists relied on pork as their main meat source. Since salt was hard to come by, curing the meat wasn't practical. Of necessity, early North Carolinians had to cook—and eat—the whole thing, lest it go to waste.

Back then, cooking outdoors over coals in a pit wasn't a pastime; it was a necessity. The cooking temperature had to be low enough to ensure that the pig cooked all the way through and to prevent the wooden rack on which the meat rested from going up in flames.

Vinegar was plentiful, as well as cheap, and served as a natural bactericide, enhancing food safety while adding flavor and masking off tastes. Ditto for peppers, fresh or dried. Besides flavor, peppers also contributed vitamin C, which helped prevent scurvy, a serious disorder that could develop in people whose diet lacked the fresh fruits and vegetables that contain vitamin C.

Add all this together and you've got basic Carolina barbecue and a sauce of vinegar, water, salt, and pepper. Eventually South Carolinians added mustard. Georgians and Virginians added tomato sauce and ketchup as available; so did North Carolinians in the western part of the state.

Historian H. L. Mencken wrote that the word *barbecue* was in common usage in Virginia and the Carolinas by 1660. There are several theories about the origin of the word. Some authorities trace it to a Caribbean Indian word, *boucan,* which means "rack of green wood." Others point to the Spanish word *barbacoa.* Some believe the word has a French root, from *de barbe à queue,* which loosely translates as "from beard to tail." At this point I don't really care. All I know is that we call it barbecue and know what is meant regardless of how it is spelled: barbecue, barbeque, bar-b-que, bar-b-cue, or BBQ (for short).

More details about the development of regional styles are included in each chapter. Suffice it to say that as the West opened up, barbecue sauce got redder, beef joined pork on the grill, and urban migration created the rib and the sauce cults.

Fast-forward three hundred years or so.

Today barbecue is sport as well as sustenance. Most of us cook barbecue for fun and because we like it, not because wild hogs are sleeping on the back porch. We eat barbecue in restaurants for an everyday treat or enjoy a big catered affair to celebrate something . . . anything.

And we also compete at cooking barbecue. Chili and barbecue cook-offs became participatory sports in the late 1960s and early '70s. Maybe the camper trailer and the interstate highway system are to blame. Those innovations made it possible for people who live otherwise normal lives to haul equipment and meats to weekend cook-offs, where they spend a couple of days in the heat tending fires, basting meat, and drinking cold beer. Only car racing makes less sense.

Yet even more astonishing, spectators come by the thousands to watch the cooks at work, eat some barbecue, drink cold beer, and take home a T-shirt commemorating the day and the event. I don't know whether those first barbecue cooks in North Carolina would be more astounded by the RVs, the fancy cookers, or the modern miracle of beer in cans.

Barbecue contests represent a full-time job for some cooks (the pros who make the circuit, hoping to rack up big prizes and big money) and an all-consuming hobby for others, who like the fun they have and the friends they make going to contests all over the country.

Barbecue contestants may haul their cooking rigs from one coast to the other, competing to earn enough points and recognition to get into one of the big contests. Accumulated points and wins allow cooks to qualify for (or be invited to) one of the big five: Houston Livestock Show, American Royal Barbecue (Kansas City Royal), Memphis in May, Jack Daniel's Invitational, and Best in the West Nugget Rib Cook-Off (see Barbecue Contests, page 167). The North Carolina Championship Pork Cook-Off is open only to winners of local pig-cooking contests sanctioned by the North Carolina Pork Council, while the cook-off called the Official North Carolina State Barbecue Championship in Tryon, North Carolina, is wide-open.

Many regional contests are sanctioned by a major barbecue association, meaning rules and a point system are established by that organization. The Kansas City Bar-becue Society and Memphis in May are two of the world's largest. Some other sanctioning organizations include the National Barbecue Association, North Carolina Pork Council, and International Barbecue Cookers Association. (See Barbecue Associations, page 167).

Some contests dare to be unsanctioned, eschewing what they feel are stupid rules or fearing dilution of regional traditions. These local or regional events are usually devoted to a specific style. This is particularly true in North Carolina, where purists don't want to compete in contests that allow other styles. They see this as a dangerous tendency toward homogenization that will eventually blur the differences and obliterate the unique characteristics of Carolina pork barbecue and other regional styles as well. Some competitive cooks do, indeed, cook Texas brisket, Memphis ribs, and Carolina whole hog in different categories within the same contest.

There's also a national association for professionals, the National Barbecue Association (NBBQA) (see Barbecue Associations, page 167).

Enthusiasts wanting to learn how to cook competition barbecue or how to judge can contact some of the associations for classes (see Classes on Barbecue, page 170).

THE FUTURE

Barbecue has a solid footing in the past, but some aficionados are worried about its future. They're not worried that barbecue will fall from favor. Years of health warnings about cholesterol and nitrites haven't cooled the national passion for it. What they're worried about, especially in the context of contests and chain restaurants, is the blurring of regional styles to the point of indistinction.

Many of the competitive cooks compete in multiple categories, cooking brisket, pork shoulder, and ribs, mixing and matching techniques, flavors, and sauces to come up with winning combinations. Ask some cooks which style they cook and you'll need a road map to plot the elements of their cuisine.

The fact is, restaurants—small, local operations—are the repositories of regional tradition, while nomadic contest cooks adopt the best ingredients and techniques they find along the way, whatever will give them a winning edge. To find real barbecue, don't go to a contest. You'll find lots of good food and lots of fun, but what you won't find is barbecue that sticks to the regional customs that have shaped and still distinguish it from one part of the country to the other.

Don't expect real barbecue at a chain restaurant. That food is manufactured to appeal to the most people, and while consistency isn't a bad thing, it isn't the real object of barbecue. In fact, consistency isn't really a requirement in barbecue. Expecting each batch of barbecue or homemade sauce to be

exactly like the one before and the one to come is like declaring that every painting by an artist should be the same.

Real barbecue is made by real people in real homes or real restaurants where they cook to please the real people around them, not contest judges, not transients stopping for a bite along the interstate or suburbanites at the shopping mall. A spotless, faux-country barbecue restaurant next to a Gap store can't be real. Barbecue is a small-town thing, and the future of barbecue—the preservation of regional distinctions—rests in the hands of folks who haven't succumbed to the WalMarting of rural America. Remember that McDonald's serves a McRib sandwich of boneless pork molded to look like ribs. That's high praise to the marketability of barbecue and a big threat to its uniquely regional characteristics. What if some kid grows up thinking *that's* barbecue?

If you love barbecue and the regional differences, eat barbecue at small, locally owned and operated restaurants at home and away. Dare to try something different and maybe even to be disappointed. Don't ever settle for chain barbecue simply because you don't know anything about what the locals eat. Ask around and count the cars in the parking lot. Other satisfied customers can't be wrong.

66 99

Southerners cling to barbecue as a source of identity and place, and to maintain a sense of individuality.

—JOHN T. EDGE, DIRECTOR, SOUTHERN FOODWAYS SYMPOSIUM, CENTER FOR THE STUDY OF SOUTHERN CULTURE, UNIVERSITY OF MISSISSIPPI

the right stuff

Low and slow is the mantra of all barbecue pit masters. Long, slow cooking with indirect heat—that is, not directly over the heat source—or over a very low fire is what makes barbecue.

Good barbecue requires good equipment. The options are many, depending on a variety of factors, including budget, cooking and storage space, the number of mouths you're feeding, and your level of enthusiasm and commitment. It is possible to spend tens of thousands of dollars on custom barbecue equipment or just a few bucks on inexpensive equipment that will also produce barbecue you can be proud of. Costs may range from $25 to $3,000 or even higher.

Types and styles of cookers range from barrels to brick-lined pits and from small grills available at discount stores to expensive designer equipment. Pros who compete in barbecue contests across the country and who also cater have portable barbecue rigs or systems on trailers. Many customize the equipment for their special needs and preferences, like smoking a whole pig or side of beef.

But most of us amateurs—including some pretty serious ones—buy something we think is big enough to meet our needs, easy enough to use, the right size for the deck or patio, and affordable. (For manufacturers' names, see Sources of Equipment, page 173.) Most of the recipes in this book are written for small to medium-size home cookers that use a combination of wood and charcoal, or gas plus wood chips for smoke seasoning.

Cookers may be constructed in a horizontal or vertical style, round or rectangular, depending on the cook's preference. With horizontal cookers, longer than they are wide, the fire can be built at one end of the grill so that the meat can be placed on the cooler side. Other cookers (usually vertical) have what are called fireboxes in which the fire burns and wafts smoke and heat over and around the meat in the cooking chamber.

Round (or kettle) cookers, except those with water pans, make it more difficult to position the meat away from the fire; in general, this shape works better for grilling. But if you've got a round cooker, don't despair. Start the fire in the middle. Once the coals have burned down to gray ash, push them to the edges, forming an area of indirect heat in the center of the grill.

Some cooks use smokers with a water pan that separates the fire from the meat, thus reducing the chances of overcooking or drying out the meat. When you use a water pan smoker, basting isn't necessary. If the flavors from a basting or "mop" liquid are desired, pour the basting liquid in the water pan, adding water as necessary to prevent the pan from cooking dry. Cooking takes longer with a water pan.

A good barbecue cooker has to have a lid and vents or a vent and chimney. They help control the fire and pull the smoke and heat over the meat to cook it. For more convenience, choose a cooker that has a fire door so you don't have to lift the cooking grate and meat whenever you need to add hot coals.

Experienced barbecuers often have several different types and sizes of cookers requiring different types of fuel. They use bigger cookers fired by wood or wood and charcoal when they've got time to spend on a brisket or pork shoulder or several racks of ribs. They may use a smaller gas- or electric-powered cooker for more casual cooking when there's less time to tend the fire.

Serious barbecuing requires a second, smaller grill that can be devoted to maintaining a steady supply of hot coals for the main cooker. It also comes in handy for grilling snacks while waiting for the barbecue to cook.

Along with a cooker (or two), you'll need cutting boards, knives and utensils, heavy gloves, squirt bottles, and fire starters. Here's a list of basic tools that will make barbecuing easier and safer.

EQUIPMENT CHECKLIST

Aluminum foil: Get heavy duty, the largest size available, for wrapping big pieces of meat to keep them warm or to store refrigerated.

Chimney fire starter: This gadget looks like a top hat without a brim and uses crumpled newspaper to start a charcoal fire quickly and efficiently, without the taste residue of chemical fire starters or treated charcoal.

Cutting board(s): Several boards (at least 1 inch thick) of varying surface area can be very helpful. If you choose only one, make sure it is large enough for holding and slicing a brisket or pork shoulder, about 10 by 16 inches. Some boards have a trench around the edge to catch runoff juices.

Electric match: These are handy for starting the fire.

Fork: A two-pronged fork is great for holding meat securely while you are carving. But it is better to use a spatula, tongs, or heat-resistant gloved hands for handling meat over the fire. Stabbing with a fork causes juices to run out.

Gloves: Different kinds are suited for different jobs. Black heat-resistant gloves are a safety bonus, especially if you're handling big pieces of meat. Plain work gloves make handling wood and charcoal a lot less messy. Latex gloves make handling raw meat more pleasant and serving cooked meat more sanitary.

Instant-read thermometer: This basic food safety tool is a must for producing good barbecue. When inserted into the meat, it immediately gives you the internal temperature, unlike traditional meat thermometers, which must be inserted in the meat during the entire cooking time. It also is handy for checking the temperature inside the cooker. Some cooks drill a small hole in the lid so they can insert their instant-read thermometer at any time. Others place an oven thermometer inside the cooker on the grill near the meat.

Knives: A large carving knife is a must for slicing cooked barbecue. A paring knife, an 8- or 10-inch chef's knife, and a boning knife also come in handy for various jobs. A Chinese cleaver is ideal for carving barbecued chicken or for chopping pulled pork or barbecued brisket.

Plastic bags: Get heavy-duty self-closing bags in a variety of sizes, mostly large. They are great for marinating meat to be cooked or for storing cooked meat.

Platters: You'll need large, heatproof platters or roasting pans that can rest on the edge of the cooker or be placed in a low oven to keep meat warm. They are also handy for switching to the Fail-Safe Technique of finishing barbecue in the oven.

Sauce mop: Used for washing dishes, the true dish mop, like a floor mop, is made of string and is perfect for swabbing meat with sauce. A pastry brush can do the same job. Keep several of both on hand. Clean them in the dishwasher.

Shovel or fire spade: One of these is a must if you're keeping a hot bed of coals going to add to the cooker. Use it for the easiest and safest way to transfer hot coals to a firebox or smoker.

Spatulas: Sturdy spatulas are great for lifting the meat so you don't have to poke fork holes in it. For large pieces of meat, you'll need two.

Squirt bottle: Keep one on hand to douse flames that get out of control. More of a necessity for grilling than for barbecuing.

Tongs: These gadgets can be a barbecue cook's best friend because they allow precise handling of the wood in the firebox and the meat on the grill. Use a separate pair of tongs for each task. For extra flexibility, get several tongs in varying lengths. A spatula and a pair of tongs may be the safest combination for moving meat around on a smoker.

using this book

Celebrating Barbecue was written to explore and explain the four great styles of American barbecue, as well as give even a beginning barbecue cook a chance to make good, possibly great, barbecue. Many of the recipes contain Fail-Safe Techniques for rescuing a potential disaster caused by inclement weather or uncooperative equipment.

Cooking temperatures, seasonings, woods and other fuels, plus techniques are explained in detail in the recipes and text. This book contains a wide range of recipes for sauces, rubs, and marinades, but many of these flavor enhancers are also available packaged (see Sources of Ingredients, page 172). Professionals often sell their concoctions to the public at cook-offs, too.

Menus, along with recipes for side dishes and desserts, are given for each regional style so cooks may create a complete and authentic barbecue feast. For those who are planning a vacation, there are lists of restaurants in each region known for their genuine barbecue methods.

True barbecue aficionados will want to learn about regional curiosities, like St. Louis barbecued snouts or Santa Maria beef tri-tip barbecue. Those specialties and others will be found in the chapter called "Wild Cards."

Rounding out the recipes are two final chapters on appetizers, side dishes, and desserts.

Concluding the book is a directory of sources where barbecue cooks can find more information on subjects that interest them. For those who want to taste and see (maybe even compete), there's a long list of cook-offs and festivals (see Barbecue Contests, page 167). For those who want to learn to cook barbecue competitively, there is a directory of pit masters who are willing to share their secrets in cooking classes (see Instructors, page 171). And since equipment is important to successful barbecue, there's a section about cookers, things to consider when buying, and a list of manufacturers (see Sources of Equipment, page 173).

It is my hope that all barbecue lovers and even expert cooks—though they may find plenty to argue with on these pages—will also find some information they can agree with and maybe even use.

SOME GENERAL GUIDELINES

The ideal smoking temperature is around 215°F, with the acceptable range between 200° and 300°F. Plan on smoking your meat for 1 to 1½ hours per pound. The outdoor temperature and wind affect the cooking time, and if you smoke on the higher end of the temperature range in each recipe, subtract about 10 minutes per pound. This means a 10-pound pork shoulder may take 15 hours to finish.

If the fire gets out of control or goes out, a Fail-Safe Technique is to wrap the meat in foil and place it in the oven at 225° to 250°F. When the meat reaches an internal temperature of 180° to 190°F, it is cooked through and probably tender. Remove the meat from the smoker (or oven, as the case may be) and let it sit for 15 to 30 minutes. This will cool it to make handling easier and allow the juices to settle.

A FINAL WORD

Barbecue is basically party food. So have fun with it. If you cook a good-quality piece of meat long enough and slowly enough, chances are you and everyone else who eats it will enjoy it.

The recipes offered here are guidelines, not blueprints for brain surgery. Don't be afraid to do things your way. Cooks who are slaves to recipes miss the point, especially within a style as open to innovation and personal preference as barbecue. There's no better way to establish your own taste profile than with barbecue.

Feel free to mix and match techniques and flavorings from different regions; nearly all the really good cooks do. Try any of the recipes in this book, add your own variations, and soon you'll be pit master of the neighborhood—or at least your own backyard.

A barbecue is always a party.

—ED "MITCH" MITCHELL, OWNER OF MITCHELL'S BARBECUE, WILSON, NORTH CAROLINA

PART TWO ★

Menu for Carolina-Style Pork Barbecue Plate

Pulled pork (pages 35 and 38) on white bread or bun

———————

South Carolina–Style Barbecue Sauce (page 43)

———————

South Carolina–Style Table Sauce or Dip (page 45)

———————

Eastern North Carolina Coleslaw (page 131)

———————

Hushpuppies (page 148)

carolina barbecue

*where vinegar, tomato, and
mustard factions wage taste wars*

In North and South Carolina, what might seem to outsiders like minor taste distinctions are major points of contention about the best sauce for barbecue. Politics and religion can be safer subjects in polite society. For personal safety, don't even think about arguing 'cue in *im*polite circles.

Around here, barbecue means pork exclusively. Chicken is chicken, ribs are ribs, but barbecue is *pork*. It is the culinary glue that binds communities and makes an event a celebration. Barbecue is the menu for gatherings as diverse as political rallies and weddings. Often barbecue restaurants are neighborhood meeting places for swapping gossip and testing the waters on candidacies or public policy issues.

The techniques for smoking pork—the whole hog almost exclusively—don't vary much from place to place. The most authentic method is still cooking directly over wood—hickory, oak, or a combination—instead of gas. While some Carolinians prefer their barbecued pig sliced, most prefer it pulled and coarsely chopped or finely minced.

But put texture questions aside—it is the sauce that truly distinguishes one intraregional genre from the other. Sauce discussions can incite territorial passions much hotter than the cooking temperature of this "low-and-slow" culinary art form.

Barbecue in the Carolinas is the most regional—and localized—of the four great schools of barbecue. It is quite likely the oldest and original American barbecue as well, dating to colonial times. Pigs, wild and domestic, were plentiful and easy to raise (or capture), and so pork was the natural pick for barbecue. A warm climate made outdoor cooking practical most of the year, giving rise to the barbecue as the best venue for a community gathering.

Colonial settlements in the Carolinas long predated modern dental care. Tooth loss was a serious health problem in the seventeenth century, explains North Carolina barbecue expert and historian Bob Garner. Serving finely chopped meat was simply considered good manners because it made chewing easier, especially in the days when pigs weren't nearly as well fed and tender as they are today. Consideration became tradition.

History accounts for sauce differences as well. When the American colonies were first settled, Europeans (including the colonists) thought tomatoes were poisonous, so they didn't use them in cooking. Vinegar, however, was a favorite ingredient for flavoring and preservation, and vinegar flavored with peppers helped to cover up the taste of less than top-quality pork in a time before refrigeration. Used as a marinade before cooking, pepper vinegar helped tenderize as well.

As time, and people, marched on, the settlers came to prize tomatoes for their color, taste, and meaty texture. This is why tomatoes are used more in barbecue sauces as you move from east to west.

Carolina sauces begin with a piquant vinegar base, not unlike the pepper sauces still used today in the Caribbean. The influence of black slave cooks on the development of barbecue cannot be overstated. Many barbecue flavor profiles in all the regions can be traced to the ingredients and techniques perfected by these involuntary settlers.

Eastern or coastal North Carolinians (or those who subscribe to this denomination of barbecue worship) prefer a peppery vinegar sauce with little, if any, tomato. Red in this style of sauce comes from spices like dried red peppers and red pepper sauce (similar to Louisiana pepper sauce, such as Tabasco), particularly the Texas Pete brand made in Winston-Salem.

In the mountainous western part of the state, known as the Piedmont, the sauce becomes thicker and less vinegary with the addition of ketchup or tomato sauce. Served at table, it is known colloquially as "dip." Some places offer browns (finely chopped charred ends) as a crispy add-in to pulled and chopped pork.

In South Carolina you'll find yellow instead of red vinegar barbecue sauces, distinguished by the addition of mustard, another vinegar sauce still used in the Caribbean today. Sauces range from yellow to orange, depending on the ratio of mustard, pepper sauce, and ketchup. Color lines aren't hard and fast, yet nowhere does the color of barbecue sauce matter so much as in the Carolinas.

There's another difference as well. In North Carolina even the coleslaw changes color from east to west. Dressed with vinegar or a thin creamy sauce in the east, coleslaw takes on a pink tinge from the addition of tomato sauce or ketchup in the Piedmont. But even in the east, the coleslaw isn't chunky textured in a creamy sauce, although the white or almost clear dressing may have a touch of mayonnaise or cream. Whether the slaw is dressed with spicy vinegar or a sweet and lightly creamy mixture, the cabbage is finely chopped or ground. No doubt that easy-chewing consideration again.

Virtually every town in the Carolinas has at least one barbecue joint. Many have several. Unlike barbecue restaurants in most other places where 'cue *is* the menu, these restaurants also offer other styles of home cooking. In addition to barbecue, there may be fried fish, fried chicken, and Brunswick stew (in North Carolina) or hash (in South Carolina). Barbecue remains the main draw, however. Other things are go-with's.

Barbecue may be served on a plate (alone or in combination with Brunswick stew or fried chicken, plus a couple of sides) or on a "tray," a paper container in which slaw and barbecue are served side by side with a hunk of cornbread or a handful of hushpuppies. Ordered as a sandwich, shredded barbecue is piled on sandwich buns or commercial (i.e., gooey) white bread and topped with a mound of slaw. Sauce or dip is added as desired.

While much of the barbecue in the Carolinas is consumed in restaurants or produced by caterers, barbecue is also a home-cooking and entertaining tradition known as a "pig picking." There are home, as well as professional, practitioners.

In the old days pits were dug in the ground and pigs cooked directly over the coals. Today, for convenience and sanitation, most pigs are cooked in brick pits or metal cookers indoors. In either case, the method remains much the same: roasting a whole hog directly over low coals for 8 to 12 hours, then pulling the meat away from the carcass, shredding or chopping it along with morsels of crisp skin or fat, and dousing it with vinegar sauce and, in some areas, dip. For home cooks a pork shoulder is easier to handle than a whole or half hog and produces respectable meat for a pickin'.

While barbecue places dot the map in both states, the following are some of the better-known ones. At most of them, cooking is done over wood or wood and charcoal for a true smoked flavor.

LEGENDARY CAROLINA BARBECUE RESTAURANTS

NORTH CAROLINA

Eastern Style

The Skylight Inn (Pete Jones' Barbeque)
"Look for the white dome"
4617 Lee St., Ayden, NC 28513
Phone: 919-746-4113

Murray's Bar-B-Que
4700 Old Poole Rd., Raleigh, NC 27610
Phone: 919-231-6258

Allen & Son Bar-B-Que (two locations)
6203 Neilhouse Rd., Chapel Hill, NC 27516
Phone and fax: 919-942-7576 (will ship barbecue)
U.S. 15-501 (between Chapel Hill and Pittsboro, just north of Haw River bridge), Pittsboro, NC 27312
Phone: 919-542-2294

Western Style
Barbecue Center, Inc.
900 N. Main, Lexington, NC 27292
Phone: 336-248-4633 (will ship barbecue)
Fax: 336-248-4647
www.barbecuecenter.com

Lexington Barbecue #1
#10 Highway 29, 70 S., Lexington, NC 27292
Phone: 336-249-9814

Eastern and Western Style Plus Soul Food
Mitchell's Barbecue and Seafood
6228 S. Ward Blvd., Wilson, NC 27893
Phone: 252-291-3808
Fax: 252-291-9336

SOUTH CAROLINA

Maurice's Gourmet Barbeque (eleven locations)
Original Piggie Park location: 1600 Charleston Hwy., West Columbia, SC 29171
Phone: 803-791-0220 (will ship barbecue)
www.mauricesbbq.com
Piggie Park Enterprises, Inc., National Headquarters
Phone: 800-628-7423
Fax: 803-791-8707

Smokin' Stokes Barbecue Restaurant
417 Stewart, Greenville, SC 29334
Phone: 864-242-9716

Carolina-Style Barbecued Whole Hog

Although most of us will never try to barbecue a whole pig, it's nice to know how it is done. And there truly is nothing quite like shards of pork pulled from a whole smoked hog. The meat is chopped and mixed with cracklings (crispy bits of skin and fat) for one of the more succulent mouthfuls you'll ever experience.

Most people call in the pros for barbecuing a whole pig, but you *can* try it at home with a 75- to 80-pound hog. That size is fairly easy to handle, although North Carolina pros like Ed Mitchell barbecue 120-pound animals. In either case, a butcher will need to special-order your hog.

This chapter also includes a recipe for pork shoulder (page 38), which is much easier for the home cook to manage.

Equipment big enough to cook a whole hog (75 to 85 pounds or larger, up to 135 pounds) is the first requirement. That means 3 by 5 to 4 by 6 feet of grill surface, two cooking grates to make turning the pig easier, and enough fuel (wood or wood and charcoal) for 12 to 20 hours of cooking time (60 to 70 pounds of charcoal). You'll also need a smaller cooker or pit in which to ignite more coals so you'll have plenty ready to add to the pit.

The next major requirement is the patience to tend the pig for that long—or longer if needed.

1 75- to 80-pound pig, head and bristles removed	1 to 2 pounds margarine, melted, or 2 bottles squeeze margarine
Carolina-style red or yellow barbecue sauce for mopping and seasoning, your choice (pages 40–43)	Carolina-style table sauce or dip, your choice (pages 44–45)

1. Have the butcher split the hog down the breast so it will lie flat or ask the butcher to separate the two halves for even easier handling. Cut off the feet or ask the butcher to do this for you. Remove any excess fat or unsightly scraps.

2. Rub or brush the pig on the meaty side with barbecue sauce. Set aside until ready to place on the fire.

3. Meanwhile, build a fire in the cooker.

4. Mound 20 pounds of wood or charcoal in the bottom of the cooker. Do not place the grate on yet. Use an electric charcoal starter (or your preferred method) to light the coals. Allow the coals to burn down until completely covered with gray ash, about 30 minutes. Spread the hot coals evenly over the bottom of the pit. Place the cooking grate over the hot coals.

5. Place the pig, meaty side down, on the grate. Close the lid. Try to maintain a cooking temperature of about 225°F; use an oven thermometer to check the heat. A less precise test: The temperature is correct if you can rest your palm on the cooker's closed lid for 2 seconds (say "one thousand one, one thousand two"). Adjust the ventilation doors on the cooker to lower the temperature (close the doors to cut off the air) or raise it (open the doors to allow more air inside).

6. Light about 5 pounds of wood or charcoal in a small cooker. After the pig has been in the large cooker for 45 minutes or so, lift the grate or open the fire door and spread the second batch of coals under the hams and shoulder. Avoid spreading them under the ribs to prevent overcooking.

7. Light about 5 pounds of wood or charcoal at a time and add additional hot coals under the hams and shoulder every 45 minutes or so for the next 5 to 6 hours. The juices should run absolutely clear when the hams or thick parts of the shoulder are pierced with a fork.

8. Now is about the time to turn the pig skin side down. When ready to turn, the skin side should be reddish brown, preferably with no charred spots.

9. This is easier to accomplish if you have a second grate and a helper or two. Wearing heat-proof gloves, place the second grate upside down on top of the pig so the pig is sandwiched between the grates. With a person at each corner, lift and turn the grates so that the pig is resting skin side down over the coals.

10. Light a final 5 to 10 pounds of wood or charcoal. While the coals burn down, brush the meat surface evenly with melted margarine or squeeze margarine. This glazes and softens the meat.

11. Next, baste the meat with barbecue sauce, allowing the sauce to puddle about 1 inch deep in the rib cavities. When the last pile of coals is covered with gray ash, spread an even layer across the entire floor of the cooker. This final layer browns and crisps the skin. Close the lid and cook 1 to 2 hours longer or as needed to crisp the skin and to allow the basting sauce to soak in and glaze.

12. The pig should be quite tender, literally falling off the bone, so that it is easy to pull off in chunks or shreds. The pig should come apart at the joints as well.

13. To "pick the pig," remove all or large sections of the pig from the grill. Using clean heavy latex gloves for food handling, peel away the fat and skin but do not discard all of it. Save some of the crispest pieces to chop into the meat for texture and flavor.

14. Some guests will want to pull their own pork from the pig. If you choose to pull and chop the meat before serving, use a heavy cleaver and chop or mince to the desired consistency. Try to

combine meat from the shoulder and ham for variety in texture. Shoulder meat is finer grained. Chop crisp fat and pieces of skin into the meat for a richer flavor.

15. Season the chopped meat with a sprinkling of red or yellow sauce for seasoning. Serve with a table sauce or dip to pour over the meat or on a sandwich.

Serves about 50.

FAIL-SAFE TECHNIQUE: *Hire a professional.*

TECHNIQUE: Direct heat (very low)	**RUB:** No
SMOKE: Hickory or oak	**MOP:** Yes
TEMPERATURE: 225° to 250°F	**SAUCE:** Peppery vinegar or peppery
TIME: 8 to 12 hours	tomato and dip for serving

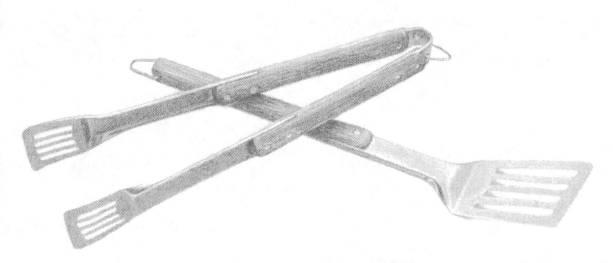

Carolina-Style Pork Shoulder

Barbecuing a shoulder instead of a whole or half hog is a lot easier to manage on most home equipment, and can even be done in a kettle-type grill. You will need to allow 8 to 10 hours. This technique is adapted from Bob Garner's formula, as outlined in his book, *North Carolina Barbecue: Flavored by Time*.

Use a fresh shoulder picnic or the cut known as Boston butt, which is actually half of a pork shoulder (not part of the ham as you might expect, given the name). You will need about 10 pounds of charcoal, a bag of wood chunks (preferably hickory), and most of the other stuff required for cooking a whole pig (page 35).

For more detailed information about pork shoulder cuts, see page 55.

1 6- to 7-pound fresh shoulder picnic or Boston butt	½ cup (1 stick) margarine, melted, or ½ cup liquid margarine, optional
1 tablespoon salt or to taste	Carolina-style table sauce or dip, your choice (pages 44–45), optional
Carolina-style red or yellow barbecue sauce for mopping and seasoning, your choice (pages 40–43)	

1. One side of the pork will have a thick layer of skin. Generously salt the other, meaty side. Let the meat rest at room temperature for 30 minutes to 1 hour.

2. Meanwhile, light 5 pounds of charcoal in the bottom of the grill and allow the coals to burn down until covered with gray ash, 20 to 30 minutes. When the coals are ready, leave 6 or 7 briquettes at the center of the grill in a circle, about the size of the meat or 10 inches in diameter. Divide the remaining briquettes into even piles and push to opposite sides of the grill.

3. Place 2 water-soaked hickory chunks on top of each side pile. When the wood chunks begin to smoke, place the cooking grate over the coals and position the pork shoulder, meat side down, in the center, directly over the circle of coals. Place the cover on the grill, leaving the ventilation holes completely open. You'll hear some sizzle and see some smoke. That's the way it should be. But if you think the coals are flaming, close the vents enough to extinguish the flames.

4. Now light about 5 pounds coals in a smaller grill or fire bucket so they'll be ready to add in

about 30 minutes. Let them burn down until covered with gray ash, then transfer about 6 hot briquettes to each side pile. Handle with fire tongs or use a spade or shovel and drop through the opening at the sides of the cooking grate (or lift the edge of the grate to add the coals). Add a couple more wood chunks on each side as well.

5. Continue adding hot briquettes and wood chunks to each side pile every 30 minutes or so to maintain the cooking temperature. Keep the lid on as much as possible.

6. After about 6 hours, turn the pork shoulder so that the meat side faces up. At this point you'll probably need to add only 4 or 5 coals on each side at 30-minute intervals to finish cooking. Don't add coals to the center.

7. Brush the meat side with barbecue sauce when adding the coals. If desired, brush with melted or liquid margarine. Continue this process for another 2 hours or until both sides—exposed meat and skin—are deep reddish brown.

8. Now test for doneness. The best way is to give the meat a good squeeze with both hands, wearing heatproof or heavy rubber gloves, of course. The meat should yield or "give" to pressure. Or stick a fork in the meat to see if it yields easily and feels soft.

9. To serve, remove the meat from the grate and place on a chopping surface, skin side up. Peel off the skin—it should come off easily in one piece—but don't throw it away. Use a sharp knife to scrape or cut away any remaining fat layer. Tear off the remaining meat in chunks by hand or use a knife.

10. Chop the meat to the desired consistency with a large knife or heavy cleaver. Add some finely chopped skin and/or fat if you like. Season the meat with additional Carolina-style barbecue sauce. Pass dip or table sauce when serving, if desired.

Serves 6 to 8.

FAIL-SAFE TECHNIQUE: *If the shoulder starts to get too dark before the meat is tender, remove it from the grill and wrap in a double thickness of foil, fat side up. Place in a 250°F oven until the meat is tender. Pull back the foil and cook an additional 30 minutes to crisp the fat side.*

TECHNIQUE: Direct heat (very low)	**RUB:** No
SMOKE: Hickory or oak	**MOP:** Yes
TEMPERATURE: 225° to 250°F	**SAUCE:** Peppery vinegar or peppery
TIME: 8 to 12 hours	tomato and dip for serving

Most Basic Eastern North Carolina (Coastal)–Style Barbecue Sauce

This is a basic sauce used for mopping during cooking or for seasoning cooked meat.

1 quart cider vinegar

2 tablespoons crushed red pepper flakes or red pepper sauce (Texas Pete is traditional brand used in North Carolina)

1 tablespoon salt or to taste

2 teaspoons black pepper or to taste

1. Combine all the ingredients in a container with a tight-fitting lid. Shake to combine.

2. Store in a tightly sealed container. No refrigeration is needed.

Makes about 1 quart.

Eastern North Carolina (Coastal)–Style Barbecue Sauce

From the coast, this is another high-acid sauce used for mopping during cooking or for seasoning cooked meat.

1 cup cider vinegar	1 tablespoon red pepper sauce
1 cup white vinegar	2 teaspoons black pepper or to taste
3 tablespoons sugar	2 teaspoons salt or to taste
1 tablespoon crushed red pepper flakes	

Combine all the ingredients in a container with a tight-fitting lid. Shake to combine. Store in the refrigerator up to 2 months.

Makes about 2½ cups.

Western North Carolina (Piedmont)–Style Barbecue Sauce

The farther west, the redder the sauce that is used for mopping during cooking or for seasoning cooked meat.

1 cup cider vinegar	1 tablespoon crushed red pepper flakes
1 cup white vinegar	1 tablespoon red pepper sauce
³/₄ cup tomato juice, tomato sauce, or ketchup	2 teaspoons black pepper or to taste
1 tablespoon sugar	2 teaspoons salt or to taste

Combine all the ingredients in a container with a tight-fitting lid. Shake to combine. Store in the refrigerator up to 2 months.

Makes about 3 cups.

Sauces get sweeter the farther west you go.

—ARDIE DAVIS, *THE GREAT BARBECUE SAUCE BOOK*

South Carolina–Style Barbecue Sauce

In South Carolina, the sauce for mopping during cooking or for seasoning cooked meat is yellow with mustard.

1 cup cider vinegar	1 tablespoon crushed red pepper flakes
1 cup white vinegar	2 teaspoons black pepper or to taste
3 tablespoons sugar	2 teaspoons salt or to taste
3/4 cup yellow mustard	

Combine all the ingredients in a container with a tight-fitting lid. Shake to combine. Store in the refrigerator up to 2 months.

Makes about 3 cups.

Western North Carolina (Piedmont)–Style Table Sauce or Dip

This sauce is used as a table sauce for pulled or chopped pork plate or sandwich, ribs, chicken, or any other smoked meat.

1½ cups cider vinegar	½ teaspoon crushed red pepper flakes or to taste
1 cup ketchup or tomato sauce	½ teaspoon red pepper sauce or to taste
⅓ cup sugar	
1 teaspoon salt	

1. Combine all the ingredients in a small saucepan over low heat. When the mixture boils, reduce the heat and simmer for 20 to 30 minutes, stirring occasionally.

2. Remove from the heat and cool. Serve at room temperature. Store in the refrigerator up to 2 months.

Makes about 2½ cups.

 Ribs are ribs, but ribs aren't barbecue in the lexicon of North Carolina.

—BOB GARNER, *NORTH CAROLINA BARBECUE*

South Carolina–Style
Table Sauce or Dip

This is a classic table sauce for pulled pork.

1½ cups yellow mustard	1 tablespoon Worcestershire sauce
5 tablespoons brown sugar	½ teaspoon cayenne pepper or to taste
¼ cup tomato paste	½ teaspoon black pepper or to taste
3 tablespoons cider vinegar	½ teaspoon garlic powder or to taste

1. Combine all the ingredients in a small saucepan over low heat. When the liquid begins to pop and bubble, lower the heat as much as possible. Simmer for about 5 minutes just to dissolve the sugar, stirring frequently.

2. Remove from the heat and cool. Serve at room temperature. Store in the refrigerator up to 2 months.

Makes about 2 cups.

Pan-Fried Chicken

Fried chicken is often served as a sidekick to barbecue at restaurants in the Carolinas.

2½ to 3 pounds small chicken drumsticks, thighs, or wings or a combination	½ teaspoon paprika
Salt as needed	Vegetable oil or shortening for frying
2 cups all-purpose flour or as needed	Cream Gravy (recipe follows), optional
2 teaspoons black pepper or to taste	

1. Rinse the chicken and place in enough heavily salted water (about 2 tablespoons salt per pint) to cover. Soak for at least 1 hour or up to overnight in the refrigerator. Drain the chicken. Submerge again in fresh water and drain again.

2. In a heavy plastic bag, combine the flour, 2 teaspoons salt, pepper, and paprika. Add the chicken, a few pieces at a time, and shake to coat evenly with the seasoned flour. Remove from the bag and place on wax paper; do not allow the pieces to touch.

3. Pour oil into a large heavy skillet to a depth of about 2 inches. Heat the oil to around 325° to 350°F.

4. Carefully slide the chicken pieces into the hot oil, a few at a time. Do not crowd the pan. The chicken should have room to float without the pieces touching. Cook the chicken until it is browned on one side, then turn and brown the other side. Do not turn more than once or twice. Drain the pieces on paper towels and keep warm.

5. To test for doneness, pierce a leg or thigh at the thickest part. The juices should run clear. Serve with cream gravy if desired. May also be served at room temperature.

Serves 6 to 8.

FAIL-SAFE TECHNIQUE: *While the chicken cooks, preheat the oven to 350°F. As the pieces are removed from the skillet, place them on a shallow baking sheet. Do not allow their sides to touch. When all the chicken is fried, place the pan in the oven for about 10 minutes. This ensures that the chicken is thoroughly cooked and will be hot when served.*

Cream Gravy

Cream or white gravy, made from pan drippings and milk or cream, is the universal go-with for Southern fried chicken, although not necessarily along with barbecue. Still, it goes against my common sense to offer a recipe for fried chicken without the option of cream gravy.

⅓ cup drippings from frying chicken or vegetable oil	1 teaspoon salt or to taste
⅓ cup leftover seasoned flour used to coat chicken or all-purpose flour	1 teaspoon black pepper or to taste
2¼ to 2½ cups milk or half-and-half	Dash of red pepper sauce, optional

1. From the skillet used for frying the chicken, pour off all but ⅓ cup of the oil used for frying. Do not discard any of the fried bits left in the bottom of the pan. If making gravy without frying a chicken first, go ahead and use a clean skillet and fresh oil, but don't expect the gravy to be as good. Browned bits from the bottom of the frying pan give it flavor and character. So does lots of black pepper.

2. Over medium heat, use a wire whisk to stir in the flour, preferably the seasoned flour used to coat the chicken. If necessary, use fresh flour but, as with the oil, the gravy won't be the same.

3. Continue stirring and cooking until the oil bubbles and froths and the flour just begins to brown. Remove the pan from the heat and slowly stir in the milk. Use the wire whisk to break up any lumps. Return the pan and reduce the heat to low. Continue stirring and cook until the gravy begins to thicken. Season to taste with the salt and pepper; add the red pepper sauce, if desired. If the gravy seems too thick, add more milk or water to thin it to the desired consistency.

Makes about 2½ cups.

Pan-Fried Fish

Fried fish is a popular menu item in barbecue restaurants, especially in the Low Country along the coast. The addition of yellow mustard to the coating gives it tang and a golden color.

12 to 16 ounces white fish fillets (catfish, trout, cod, or other firm-fleshed fish), without skin	1 teaspoon salt or to taste
	1 teaspoon black pepper or to taste
	$^1/_8$ teaspoon cayenne pepper or to taste, optional
1 cup milk	
1 tablespoon yellow mustard	Oil for frying
$^1/_2$ cup yellow cornmeal or as needed	Lemon slices or bottled tartar sauce, optional
$^1/_2$ cup all-purpose flour or as needed	

1. Rinse and dry the fish. In a shallow pan or dish, combine the milk and mustard, stirring to mix well. Add the fish in a single layer, if possible, so that it is covered with milk on all sides. Refrigerate about 30 minutes.

2. In another shallow pan or dish (or a plastic bag), combine the cornmeal, flour, salt, and black pepper; add the cayenne, if desired. Stir with a fork or shake the bag to evenly distribute the ingredients. Coat the fish fillets on all sides with the cornmeal mixture or place a few pieces at a time in the bag and shake to coat evenly. Set the coated fish aside on wax paper while the oil heats.

3. Pour enough oil into a large heavy skillet so that the fish can float, 1 to 2 inches deep, depending on the thickness of the fillets. Heat the oil to about 370°F.

4. Carefully slide the fish, a few pieces at a time, into the hot oil. Cook until golden on one side, 3 to 4 minutes. Turn the fillets and cook the other side 2 to 3 minutes or until golden. Do not let the fillets touch while frying; they will float when done. Remove them to a platter lined with absorbent paper and keep warm.

5. Continue until all the fillets are cooked. Serve hot with lemon slices to squeeze over the fish or with tartar sauce on the side.

Serves 4 to 5.

Brunswick Stew

This thick chicken stew was originally made from game, such as squirrel. It is another typical side dish often served with Carolina-style barbecue and is also served as a main dish. Some restaurants even offer what they call Q Stew (page 50), which is Brunswick stew topped with barbecue.

1 2½- to 3-pound chicken	1 10-ounce package frozen whole-kernel corn
1 pound boneless pork, such as shoulder or fresh ham	¼ cup all-purpose flour or as needed, optional
2 onions, coarsely chopped	
3 medium potatoes, peeled and cubed	2 teaspoons salt or to taste
1 14½-ounce can crushed tomatoes	1 teaspoon black pepper or to taste
1 10-ounce package frozen lima beans	1 teaspoon red pepper sauce or to taste

1. Rinse the chicken inside and out; allow to drain. Rinse the pork and wipe dry. Place the chicken and pork in a large stewpot or Dutch oven. Add water to cover, about 6 cups.

2. Bring liquid to a boil, reduce the heat, cover, and simmer 1½ to 2 hours or until the pork is tender. Remove the chicken and pork from the broth; cool enough to handle. Remove the chicken meat from the carcass, discarding skin and bones. Chop or shred the chicken meat and return to the broth. Cut the pork into bite-size pieces or shred and add to the broth.

3. Add the onions, potatoes, tomatoes, and lima beans. Cook over low heat until the lima beans are soft, about 30 minutes. Remove about 1 cup vegetables (mainly potatoes and lima beans) from the broth. Place in a blender and puree, or mash with a potato masher; return to the stewpot. This helps thicken the stew.

4. Stir in the corn and simmer about 30 minutes, uncovered, to reduce the liquid slightly. For an even thicker consistency, ladle about ½ cup liquid from the stewpot; cool 10 minutes. Stir the flour into the cooled broth, using a whisk to prevent lumps. Gradually stir the dissolved flour into the stew and cook at least 5 minutes longer or until the desired consistency.

5. Add the salt, pepper, and red pepper sauce to taste.

Serves 6 to 8.

Q Stew

In North Carolina barbecue restaurants, Brunswick stew is topped with a nest of shredded or chopped pork barbecue, along with some cracklings for an added flavor boost. At home it is a great way to use up the last bits of the weekend's pulled pork or other barbecue.

Serve with Piedmont or coastal vinegar barbecue sauce and Piedmont dip (or table sauce).

4 tablespoons chopped barbecue pork skin (cracklings) or crisp pieces of fat, optional

4 bowls Brunswick Stew (page 49)

3 to 4 cups chopped Carolina-Style Pork Shoulder (page 38)

Mix 1 tablespoon pork cracklings into each bowl of stew, if desired. Top each bowl with a mound of finely chopped barbecue.

Makes 4 servings.

 Chopped-up barbecue was considered polite because so many people had bad teeth.

—BOB GARNER, *NORTH CAROLINA BARBECUE*

Barbecue Salad

This is as close to a "diet plate" as I found while eating barbecue in North Carolina. It can be adapted for other barbecue besides pork.

2 to 3 cups torn iceberg lettuce or American-style salad blend

1 small tomato, sliced thick

$\frac{1}{4}$ cup Carolina-style red or yellow barbecue sauce, your choice (pages 40–43)

$\frac{1}{4}$ to $\frac{1}{2}$ cup grated yellow cheese

1 to 2 cups chopped Carolina-Style Pork Shoulder (page 38) or other leftover barbecue

$\frac{1}{4}$ cup favorite Carolina-style table sauce or dip, your choice (pages 44–45)

Toss together the lettuce, tomato, and vinegar barbecue sauce. Add the cheese and the pork, mounding most of the meat on top. Drizzle some of the table sauce or dip on the meat. Serve the remaining table sauce on the side and add as desired.

Serves 1 to 2.

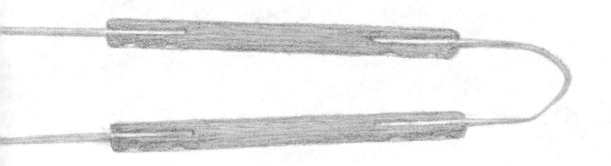

Menu for Memphis-Style Rib Plate

Dry or Wet ribs (pages 57 and 58)

Tennessee-Style Barbecue Sauce (page 68)

Barbecue Baked Beans (page 137)

Mustard Potato Salad (page 142)

Creamy Coleslaw (page 133)

memphis barbecue

Barbecued ribs are a phenomenon of urban migration. Barbecue came to town after the Civil War when displaced former slaves and their descendants were looking for new, nonagricultural ways of life. The trickle from the rural to the urban South and Midwest increased considerably in the early half of the twentieth century as it became more profitable for landowners to use machines instead of people for picking cotton.

Ribs—easier to handle and less time, space, and fuel consuming than a pit-barbecued whole hog—quickly became treasured in cities like Memphis, St. Louis, and Chicago, which attracted a large number of African-Americans.

Nowhere are ribs more dominant than in Memphis. Here barbecue and Beale Street jazz are as emblematic as pastries and Mozart symphonies in Vienna, especially in spring, when the giant barbecue contest known as Memphis in May draws the focus of the barbecue world to this Mississippi River city. More than three hundred barbecue cooking teams converge on a downtown city park to rub, mop, smoke, sauce, slice, and eat for three days.

Memphis in May is probably the most celebrated of all cook-offs, drawing barbecue experts (or would-be experts) from all over the United States and around the world. Not surprisingly, boisterous, outdoorsy Australians love barbecue and take readily to the assertive flavors and demanding techniques. Unlike many of the contests in the Carolinas, which are devoted exclusively to the traditional style, MIM has categories for everything from whole hog to beef brisket.

Yet barbecue (*always* pork in Memphis) remains a serious business year-round. So does the debate about whether ribs are better wet (sticky, with lots of sauce) or dry (seasoned and smoked, with sauce on the side). While this may seem like a minor issue to someone outside the Memphis barbecue collective, it is (like most group issues) a very big deal on the inside.

Charlie Vergos, proprietor of the fifty-year-old downtown restaurant The Rendezvous, is a member of the dry school of thought, believing that too much sauce covers up the taste of the rib meat. The Rendezvous is hard to find, but don't be afraid to ask. Everyone in town knows the directions, and no one who's ever been there forgets. Even tourists, at least those with grease on their fingers, can help out.

Inside, the restaurant smells as smoky as the ribs. Table service is genteel, unlike that in typical barbecue joints, where attitudes range from casual to downright surly and ordering at the counter is the rule. Savory spices and smoke complement the pork's natural sweetness. Sauce is available on the side. Those of the purist persuasion view sauce as strictly optional, but theirs seems to be the minority opinion.

Corky's restaurants have a huge following as well. A suburban phenomenon,

Corky's offers drive-through locations. The casual interiors don't have the sooty glaze of The Rendezvous, but the smoky aromas are no less enticing. Don't expect courtly service, though. That isn't to say you won't be treated nice—you will—but Corky's doesn't have the atmosphere of the Old South, as does The Rendezvous.

That's just as well because Corky's ribs are falling-off-the-bone tender, gooey, and messy. It's hard to mind your manners while enjoying a mess of wet ribs. You'll go through a lot of napkins. The combination of meat, sauce, and smoke makes for a tender, succulent rib with a touch of sweet. This style predominates in Memphis.

Ribs are the ultimate barbecue for many connoisseurs. Good ribs are what many barbecue cooks long to produce; great ribs are the Holy Grail, storied and elusive. Ask the experts and they'll tell you that getting the right cut of ribs is at least as important for success as technique.

Spareribs (from the belly of the pig, behind the shoulder) are traditionally used for barbecue, cooked by the slab and cut into individual ribs after cooking. There is meat on top of the bones and between. A typical slab contains eleven to thirteen long bones. Typical supermarket-quality spareribs are the least expensive and the least satisfactory for barbecuing.

Experienced barbecue cooks prefer what are known as three-and-down St. Louis cut ribs, trimmed of excess fat and the brisket bone removed. A full rack or slab should weigh 3 pounds or less. Kansas City cut ribs are another variation. They are trimmed even more than the St. Louis cut. Top-quality ribs often must be special-ordered from a good butcher.

Baby back ribs, also called loin ribs, have become popular in recent years. Shorter and smaller than spareribs, these come from the loin and are meatier, leaner, more tender, and also considerably more expensive.

Still another cut, called country-style ribs, aren't really ribs. More like fatty pork chops than ribs, they come from the blade end of the loin.

Rib experts say "skinning" spare ribs is important for optimum flavor and tenderness (see Memphis-Style Dry Ribs, page 57, for instructions). If you ever eat untrimmed ribs, you quickly become a believer in removing the thin but tough, whitish-clear membrane from the bony side of the rack, no matter how tedious the job. Better yet, see if you can talk your butcher into doing it. Eating unskinned ribs nearly always requires a vigorous follow-up session with a toothpick or dental floss. Besides making chewing easier, peeling off the membrane allows more fat to drip away and promotes penetration of the meat by seasonings and sauce.

While whole hog barbecue has stayed largely on the farm, not all barbecue in Memphis is ribs. There's considerable pork shoulder as well, served sliced, pulled, or chopped in chunks (not chopped fine, as in the Carolinas). The sauce profile is red and sweet, with some tang thrown in. Sauces are relatively subtle compared to the vinegary style of the Carolinas, the spice of Kansas City, and the savory smoke of Texas.

There's a strong argument to be made that pork shoulder is the perfect meat for barbecue. This cut is, quite simply, hard to ruin. Even beginners can produce good barbecue with pork shoulder. Unlike ribs, it is relatively inexpensive, and unlike brisket, it has more fat to keep it juicy.

The pork shoulder is the entire front leg and shoulder of a hog, usually divided into two cuts, the Boston butt and the picnic. Don't let the "b" word fool you. The butt is from the upper part of the front shoulder.

A whole pork shoulder usually weighs between 12 and 16 pounds. It will have a bone and joint plus lots of fat, the key to good barbecue. During long hours of smoking, the fat melts into the meat to keep it moist and flavorful.

If the pork shoulder has been divided, the Boston butt and the picnic will usually weigh 6 to 8 pounds each. Of the two, the Boston butt has less bone. Both cuts can be ordered boneless, but barbecue aficionados don't recommend cooking boneless. A big chunk of pork without a bone just doesn't taste as good when it comes off the grill.

Whether sliced or pulled, pork shoulder is the ultimate Fail-Safe. When you get down to the end of the shoulder or want to find something to do with small pieces of trimming, consider another Memphis specialty, barbecue spaghetti.

This dish is not just leftover barbecue tossed with spaghetti and barbecue sauce. Frank Vernon's Bar B Que Shop is considered the spiritual home of barbecue spaghetti, although restaurants all over town serve it. Frank won't say exactly what's in it—only that lacing the sauce base with barbecue drippings is the key. He attributes the recipe to Brady Vinson, a former railroad cook, from whom he bought the business.

In the end, though, Memphis barbecue is mostly about ribs. No matter which style you prefer, you'll be in good company in Memphis. The kind of ribs you like best, as with most barbecue, is what you grew up on (or at least first tasted). That kind of imprinting is hard, if not impossible, to alter. Still, it never hurts to try something different. Satisfy the urge at one of the following Memphis spots.

LEGENDARY MEMPHIS BARBECUE RESTAURANTS

The Bar B Que Shop
1782 Madison Ave., Memphis, TN 38104
Phone: 901-272-1277
www.dancingpigs.com

Corky's (multiple locations)
5259 Poplar Ave., Memphis, TN 38119
Phone: 800-926-7597 (CORKYS) or
    901-685-9744 (will ship barbecue)
www.corkysbbq.com
E-mail: bbqinfo@corkysbbq.com

Neely's Bar-B-Que (two locations)
670 Jefferson, Memphis, TN 38105
Phone: 901-521-9798 (will ship sauce
    and seasonings)
5700 Mount Moriah St., Memphis, TN
    38115
Phone: 901-795-4177
Fax: 901-521-7252
www.memphisbarbeque.com
E-mail: neelybarbq@aol.com

The Rendezvous Barbecue Restaurant
52 S. Second Street, Memphis, TN
    38103
Phone: 901-523-2746
Fax: 901-525-7688
For shipping: 901-522-8840
www.hogsfly.com

Memphis-Style Dry Ribs

While ribs are the signature of Memphis, all of Tennessee and the rest of the South cooks ribs too, as well as pork shoulder and the whole hog. Here's how.

This style is technically similar to that of The Rendezvous restaurant in that the ribs aren't sauced before serving. Serve the sauce on the side, if at all.

2 full racks of three-and-down pork spareribs (about 6 pounds) (see page 78)	Memphis Mop (page 66), optional
	Memphis-Style Barbecue Sauce (page 67), optional
The South Shall Rub Again (page 65)	

1. To skin the ribs, use a blunt knife (even a screwdriver) to loosen the membrane and lift it from the bones. Once you get started, your fingers are the best tool for getting under the membrane to tear it away. Do this before seasoning the ribs with a rub or mop.

2. Coat the ribs generously with the rub. Press the spices into the meat with your fingers or the back of a spoon. Allow the ribs to come to room temperature, about 1 hour.

3. Meanwhile, prepare a fire by lighting wood or a combination of wood and charcoal in the firebox of a cooker or at the end of a barrel smoker opposite the end with the vent or chimney. Or light the coals in a water smoker. Or preheat a gas smoker/grill.

4. When the fire has burned down to glowing embers or the coals are covered with gray ash, place the ribs, meaty side up, on the grate but not directly over the coals. Or place a full pan of water over the coals or hot lava rocks, then add the grate and ribs.

5. Cover the cooker and allow the ribs to smoke for 1 hour. The temperature inside the cooker should be between 225° and 250°F. Add coals as needed to maintain it. If desired, baste the ribs with the mop. Continue cooking 2 to 3 hours, turning (and basting, if desired) every 30 minutes or so, until they are tender and the meat pulls away from the bone.

6. About 15 minutes before removing the ribs from the cooker, sprinkle the meaty side with additional rub. Cook long enough, meaty side up, for the rub to melt or cook into the ribs.

7. To serve, slice the ribs between the bones into individual pieces. If desired, serve with the barbecue sauce on the side.

Serves about 4.

FAIL-SAFE TECHNIQUE: *Preheat the oven to 200°F. Place the seasoned ribs on baking sheets in the oven for about 3 hours. This tenderizes and cooks them while setting the spices. The ribs won't brown at this temperature; that's OK. During the last hour the ribs are in the oven, prepare a fire by lighting wood or a combination of wood and charcoal. Allow the coals to burn down to low or medium-low, with a heavy layer of ash. Place the ribs directly over the low coals. Baste on all sides with the mop, if desired, and cook until browned, turning occasionally to cook evenly, about 30 minutes. Sprinkle the meaty side with rub and cook, meaty side up, about 15 minutes longer.*

TECHNIQUE: Indirect heat	**RUB:** Yes
SMOKE: Hickory or oak	**MOP:** Optional
TEMPERATURE: 225° to 250°F	**SAUCE:** None or on the side
TIME: 2 to 3 hours, up to 4 hours	

Memphis-Style Wet Ribs

Have plenty of napkins handy for these ribs. They are sticky and messy and altogether delicious.

2 full racks of three-and-down pork spareribs (about 6 pounds) (see page 78)	Memphis Mop (page 66)
	Tennessee-Style Barbecue Sauce (page 68)
The South Shall Rub Again (page 65)	

1. To skin the ribs, use a blunt knife (even a screwdriver) to loosen the membrane and lift it from the bones. Once you get started, your fingers are the best tool for getting under the membrane to tear it away. Do this before seasoning the ribs with a rub or mop.

2. Coat the ribs generously with the rub. Press the spices into the meat with your fingers or the back of a spoon. Allow the ribs to come to room temperature, about 1 hour.

3. Meanwhile, prepare a fire by lighting wood or a combination of wood and charcoal in the firebox of a cooker or at the end of a barrel smoker opposite the end with the vent or chimney. Or light the coals in a water smoker. Or preheat a gas smoker/grill.

4. When the fire has burned down to glowing embers or the coals are covered with gray ash, place the ribs, meaty side up, on the grate but not directly over the coals. Or place a full pan of water over the coals or hot lava rocks, then add the grate and ribs.

5. Cover the cooker and smoke the ribs for 1 hour. The temperature inside the cooker should be between 225° and 250°F. Add coals as needed to maintain it. Baste the ribs with the mop and continue cooking 2 to 3 hours, basting every 30 minutes or so, until they are tender and the meat pulls away from the bone.

6. Brush the ribs generously on all sides with the barbecue sauce and cook 30 minutes longer to glaze, meaty side down.

7. To serve, slice the ribs between the bones into individual pieces.

Serves about 4.

FAIL-SAFE TECHNIQUE: *Preheat the oven to 200°F. Place the seasoned ribs on baking sheets in the oven for about 3 hours. This tenderizes and cooks them while setting the spices. The ribs won't brown at this temperature; that's OK. During the last hour the ribs are in the oven, prepare a fire by lighting wood or a combination of wood and charcoal. Allow the coals to burn down to low, with a heavy layer of ash. Place the ribs directly over the low coals. Baste with the mop and cook, turning occasionally to cook evenly, about 30 minutes. Brush the ribs generously on all sides with the barbecue sauce and cook 30 minutes longer to glaze.*

TIP: *For extra-sticky, falling-off-the-bone-tender Memphis-style wet ribs, before brushing the ribs with barbecue sauce, set each rack on a piece of foil large enough to loosely cover it. Generously brush all sides of the ribs with sauce and wrap loosely, meaty side up. Place the wrapped ribs directly over low coals and cook for 15 to 30 minutes so that the sauce soaks in. The ribs will be very messy.*

TECHNIQUE: Indirect heat	RUB: Yes
SMOKE: Hickory or oak	MOP: Yes
TEMPERATURE: 225° to 250°F	SAUCE: Yes
TIME: 2 to 3 hours, up to 4 hours	

THE BASICS

Memphis-Style Barbecued Pork Shoulder

When barbecue isn't ribs in Tennessee, it is still pork. For pulled pork without going whole hog, use a piece of pork shoulder, often sold in meat markets as Boston butt. Serve it sliced for polite eating with knife and fork, or pulled in hunks for eating with fingers (the traditional way). It also makes great sandwiches with coleslaw.

The South Shall Rub Again (page 65)

1 4- to 5-pound pork butt or shoulder roast

Memphis Mop (page 66), optional

Tennessee-Style Barbecue Sauce
    (page 68)

8 to 10 sandwich buns, optional

Creamy Coleslaw (page 133), optional

Red pepper sauce, such as Tabasco or
    Texas Pete, optional

1. Sprinkle a generous layer of the rub on all surfaces of the pork roast. Using your hands (preferably gloved to prevent spices from burning your eyes or skin), rub the mixture into the meat. Wrap the meat in plastic wrap and refrigerate for at least 3 hours or overnight.

2. Remove the pork from the refrigerator and unwrap about 1 hour before placing on the grill, to let it come to room temperature.

3. Soak the wood chips in water at least 1 hour before you begin grilling.

4. Prepare a fire by lighting wood or a combination of wood and charcoal in the firebox of a cooker or at the end of a barrel smoker opposite the end with the vent or chimney. Or preheat a gas smoker/grill.

5. When the fire has burned down to glowing embers or the coals are covered with gray ash, place the pork, fat side up, on the grate but not directly over the coals. Or place a full pan of water over the coals or hot lava rocks, then position the grate and add the pork.

6. Cover the cooker and smoke the pork shoulder, turning it every hour or so, until it is tender and the internal temperature reaches 195°F on an instant-read thermometer, 4 to 6 hours.

7. Tend the fire by adding wood (or wood embers from a separate fire) or coals to keep it from going out and to keep the temperature inside the cooker between 225° and 300°F. If using a mop, brush it on when turning the pork or after tending the fire. Add soaked chips as needed to maintain the smoke flavoring.

8. Remove the pork from the cooker and allow it to rest, covered loosely with foil, for about 15 minutes. Trim off the exterior skin and fat and slice very thin. (For more detailed instructions on trimming and slicing pork shoulder, see Carolina-Style Pork Shoulder, page 38).

9. For pulled pork, wearing heavy rubber gloves (if the pork is just off the cooker) or latex food-handling gloves, peel away and discard the skin layer. Then, with your fingers or two forks, pull the pork into thin pieces about 1 by 2 inches.

10. For sandwiches, pile slices or pulled pieces between buns with a generous slather of barbecue sauce and a crown of coleslaw.

11. Make sure red pepper sauce is handy for those who want to sprinkle it on their sandwiches.

Serves 8 to 10.

FAIL-SAFE TECHNIQUE: *If the shoulder starts to get too brown, remove it from the cooker and wrap in a double thickness of aluminum foil. Roast in a 300°F oven until tender.*

TECHNIQUE: Indirect heat	**RUB:** Yes
SMOKE: Hickory or oak	**MOP:** Optional
TEMPERATURE: 250° to 300°F	**SAUCE:** Yes, if making sandwiches
TIME: 4 to 6 hours	

Tennessee-Style Barbecued Whole Pig

There are still occasions for pig-pickings in Tennessee. Here's a method for whole hog (instead of split Carolina-style) smoked with indirect heat to produce a golden brown whole carcass that makes a dramatic presentation with an apple in its mouth.

1 75- to 85-pound whole hog	50 to 75 white sandwich buns
1 gallon vegetable oil	2 gallons Tennessee-Style Barbecue Sauce (page 68)
1 pound salt or to taste	
1 pound pepper or to taste	2 gallons Creamy Coleslaw (page 133)
2 gallons Whole Pig Basting Sauce (page 66)	Red pepper sauce, such as Tabasco or Texas Pete, optional
1 apple, optional	

1. Build a fire at one end of a smoker large enough to hold a whole hog. You can use charcoal or wood or a combination. Hickory wood or chips are particularly good for flavoring barbecued pig. Be sure you have enough fuel (at least 20 pounds) to keep a steady temperature of about 300°F.

2. Rinse the hog inside and out. Trim away any loose skin or fat. Remove the kidneys if the butcher hasn't done this for you. Pry open the mouth and insert a small log or large stick.

3. Rub the pig, inside and out, with oil. Rub the cavity with salt and pepper. Locate the tenderloins (alongside the spine from the rear end to about the middle of the pig). Cover them with aluminum foil and secure the foil with toothpicks. The tenderloins are very tender and choice and need to be protected from burning; save them for the cook and helpers when the pig is done. Wrap the ears, feet, and snout in foil.

4. When the fire burns down to about 350°F, place the pig in the smoker with the front end nearest the heat source. After the first hour, brush with the basting sauce every hour or so during the cooking time. Smoke at about 250° to 300°F for 5 to 6 hours or until the shoulders reach an internal temperature of 90° to 100°F on an instant-read thermometer.

5. Turn the pig (it's easier to turn the grate with the pig on it) so the ham (rear) end is nearest the heat. Mop generously with the baste. Using an instant-read thermometer, check the internal temperature of the meat. When the hams reach 110° to 120°F, remove the foil so the ears and snout will brown.

6. Continue smoking and basting until the internal temperature reaches 165°F, 12 to 15 hours. Keep the heat low enough to prevent burning and be prepared to cook until the meat is done throughout. Worry less about overcooking than undercooking.

7. Remove the pig from the smoker. Remove the log or stick from the hog's mouth and replace with an apple. Strip away the skin and pull the meat away from the carcass. Pull and/or slice the meat.

8. For sandwiches, serve between buns with a generous slather of barbecue sauce and a crown of coleslaw.

9. Make sure red pepper sauce is handy for those who want to sprinkle it on their sandwiches.

Serves 50 to 75.

FAIL SAFE TECHNIQUE: *Hire a professional.*

THE BASICS

TECHNIQUE: Indirect heat	**RUB:** Yes
SMOKE: Hickory or oak	**MOP:** Yes
TEMPERATURE: 225° to 300°F	**SAUCE:** Yes
TIME: 12 to 15 hours, up to 20 hours	

Oven-Smoked
Baby Back Ribs

These ribs are so good, you'll never believe they didn't come from a smoker! Long hours of slow roasting gives them the tenderness of smoked ribs, and the addition of some wood shavings gives them plenty of smoke flavor. Grilling or broiling at the end gives them a nice finish. This technique works best with meaty baby backs. Be sure and use top-quality ribs; a rack of bony spares from the typical supermarket meat department won't have much but bone for you to chew on. Seek out a butcher or check with a meat supply house to get the best.

There's one drawback to this method: The ribs need to go into the oven for 8 to 12 hours. If you're using wood for a smoky flavor, be prepared for the house to smell like the chimney's blocked.

2 full racks of baby back ribs
    (about 3½ pounds)

4 to 5 hickory or oak wood chips,
    soaked in water for at least 1 hour,
    or ½ cup hickory or oak shavings
    for stovetop smoker

Salt and pepper to taste

Tennessee-Style Barbecue Sauce
    (page 68)

1. To skin the ribs, use a blunt knife (even a screwdriver) to loosen the membrane and lift it from the bones. Once you get started, your fingers are the best tool for getting under the membrane to tear it away. Do this before seasoning the ribs with a rub or mop.

2. Preheat the oven to 200°F. Spread the soaked wood chips in the bottom of a broiler pan (if using wood shavings, sprinkle them in the bottom of a stovetop smoker). Position a rack in the pan over the chips.

3. Rinse and dry the ribs and place them on the rack. Roast in the oven for 8 to 12 hours, depending on the thickness of the meat and the desired tenderness. The meat will fall off the bone at the end of the long cooking time.

4. It's OK to check the ribs now and then, but it's not really necessary. They won't burn at such a low temperature, so just let 'em roast in peace.

5. To finish the ribs for serving, you can glaze them on an outdoor grill (recommended) or under a hot broiler (if that's the only option).

6. Season the ribs generously with salt and pepper to taste. Brush with the barbecue sauce.

7. To finish on a grill, prepare a fire by lighting wood or a combination of wood and charcoal during the last hours the ribs are in the oven. Allow the coals to burn down to low, with a heavy layer of ash. Place the seasoned ribs directly over the low coals. Grill, turning occasionally to cook evenly, about 15 to 20 minutes.

8. To finish under a broiler, preheat the broiler. Place the seasoned ribs about 6 inches from the heat source and broil until the edges brown, 5 to 10 minutes. Turn the ribs and broil another 5 to 10 minutes.

9. Slice the ribs between the bones into individual pieces, or divide each rack and serve, uncut, as half racks. Serve with additional sauce, if desired.

Serves 4.

The South Shall Rub Again

This spice blend will rub pork the right way. It can be adjusted toward the savory side by backing off on the amount of sugar.

3 tablespoons granulated garlic	2 teaspoons ground sage
3 tablespoons paprika	2 teaspoons ground ginger
3 tablespoons sugar	1 teaspoon ground cumin
2 tablespoons salt	1 teaspoon dry mustard
1 tablespoon black pepper	½ to 1 teaspoon cayenne pepper

In an airtight container with a lid, combine all the ingredients. Shake to mix well. This will keep up to a year in a cool, dark place.

Makes about 2½ cups.

Memphis Mop

Use this mop to baste pork ribs or shoulder during smoking. Add the molasses to it if you like sweet ribs or omit for a tangy, more savory mop. Add the pepper sauce for extra heat. If you like your ribs or shoulder sweet and hot, add both.

2 cups cider vinegar	1 tablespoon black pepper
1/4 cup (1/2 stick) margarine or butter	1/4 cup molasses, optional
2 tablespoons yellow mustard	1/2 to 1 teaspoon red pepper sauce, optional
1 tablespoon salt	

In a small saucepan, combine the vinegar, margarine or butter, mustard, salt, and pepper. If desired, add the molasses and/or red pepper sauce. Bring to a boil over low heat. Reduce the heat to very low and simmer about 10 minutes.

Makes about 3 cups.

Whole Pig Basting Sauce

This recipe makes enough to baste a whole hog while you're smoking it (cooking it over indirect heat).

2 cups red wine vinegar	1 tablespoon salt
2 cups vegetable oil	1 tablespoon black pepper
1/2 cup yellow mustard	

Combine the ingredients, mixing well. Refrigerate until needed.

Makes about 1 quart.

Memphis-Style
Barbecue Sauce

This sauce is the characteristic mustardy version, with some brown sugar and vinegar for sweet and sour tang, plus mustard and some pepper for bite. Serve it on the side with dry ribs or pork shoulder.

2 cups ketchup	1 teaspoon Worcestershire sauce or to taste
1/2 cup packed brown sugar	
1/4 cup yellow mustard	1 teaspoon garlic salt or to taste
1/4 cup cider vinegar	1 teaspoon red pepper sauce or to taste
2 teaspoons black pepper	Juice from 1/2 lemon or to taste

Combine all the ingredients except the lemon juice in a small nonreactive saucepan. Stir well and simmer over low heat for about 30 minutes, stirring occasionally. Add the lemon juice, stir, and adjust the seasonings to taste. Cook 5 minutes longer. Store refrigerated up to 2 weeks.

Makes about 3 cups.

Tennessee-Style Barbecue Sauce

This sauce is a bit sweeter, a bit less mustardy than Memphis-style sauce. It is more the quintessential Southern style. Serve with "wet" ribs or pork shoulder.

1 cup ketchup	1 tablespoon paprika
1 8-ounce can tomato sauce	1½ teaspoons onion salt
1 cup packed brown sugar	1 teaspoon dry mustard
1 cup cider vinegar	1 to 2 teaspoons red pepper sauce or
1 tablespoon Worcestershire sauce	to taste

Combine all the ingredients in a small saucepan. Cook and stir over low heat until the sugar melts and the ingredients are blended. Lower the heat and simmer about 10 minutes. Store refrigerated up to 2 weeks.

Makes about 3½ cups.

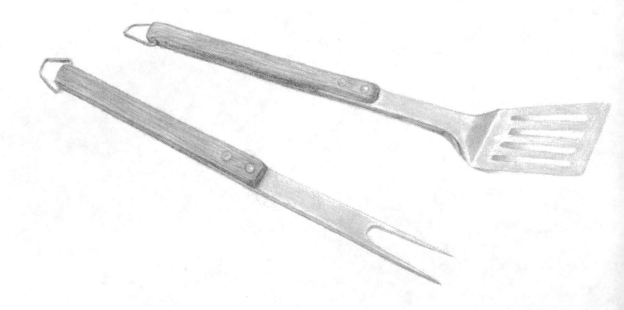

Barbecue Spaghetti

This is a traditional dish in some Memphis barbecue joints. Of course, in that part of the barbecue world, the leftover 'cue of choice is pork. But this would work wonders on a plate of pasta when made with barbecued chicken, beef, lamb, or crumbled browned ground beef or bulk sausage.

1 tablespoon vegetable oil	Pinch of ground allspice
1 cup chopped onion	Pinch of ground cloves
1 green bell pepper, chopped	Pinch of ground cinnamon
2 cups Tennessee-Style Barbecue Sauce (page 68) or your choice of bottled barbecue sauce	2 cups pulled pork or shredded barbecue beef, chicken, or lamb
½ cup bottled spaghetti sauce or tomato sauce	1 16-ounce package thin spaghetti, cooked

Heat the oil in a large saucepan. Add the onion and bell pepper. Cook over medium heat until the onion is soft. Stir in the barbecue sauce, spaghetti or tomato sauce, allspice, cloves, cinnamon, and pork. Bring to a boil, lower the heat, and simmer, stirring frequently to prevent sticking, about 10 minutes. Stir in the spaghetti and heat through.

Serves 4 to 6.

VARIATION: *Substitute cooked ground beef or bulk sausage for the pulled pork. Crumble 1 pound ground beef or bulk pork sausage into a saucepan. Cook until the meat loses its color. Proceed with the recipe, omitting the oil.*

Menu for Texas-Style Beef Barbecue (or Combo) Plate

Texas Beef Brisket Barbecue (page 75)

Barbecued Sausage (page 80)

Smoky Texas Ribs (page 78)

Lone Star Barbecue Sauce (page 88)

Cowboy Pinto Beans (page 138)

Potato Salad with Mayonnaise and Hard-Cooked Eggs (page 141)

Creamy Coleslaw (page 133)

texas barbecue

here's the beef!

In Texas, barbecue is beef—beef brisket, to be exact. The pièce de résistance, a tour de force, brisket is the measuring stick for any barbecue joint or individual who thinks he or she can cook Texas style. Notoriously high maintenance, brisket, more than any other cut of meat, requires low and slow cooking. Even slicing brisket is considerably more exacting than pulling and chopping pork.

Of course, Texans are famous for ribs too. Pork ribs, but no one dwells too much on that fact. Texas is, after all, a cattle state. That explains its allegiance to brisket despite the meat's inherent difficulties. Nevertheless, ribs, sausage, ham, and chicken—even cabrito (young goat)—can be found on a two- or three-meat combo plate in various parts of the state. But the menu begins with brisket. Everything else is an add-on.

Like most forms of barbecue, the art of the perfect brisket emerged from the practices of early settlers. Within the state there are differences resulting from various influences. Germans, who have a strong tradition of smoking meats and making sausage, settled much of central Texas and the Hill Country. Their European meat-smoking techniques combined with flavor influences from south of the border account for many of the characteristics of Texas barbecue.

The flavor of barbecue in East Texas, however, tends to be more like that in states of the

Deep South, since Louisiana and Arkansas are next door. And Texas was a favorite destination for disillusioned Tennesseans who felt crowded as their state was settled or whose legal or financial troubles dictated the need for a new address. Davy Crockett and his band of Tennesseans were among those who fought at the Alamo, so similarities between Texas and Southern barbecue were bound to occur. Texas barbecue sauce isn't as sweet as that of Tennessee or the rest of the South, but the tomato base, along with a serious mustard signature à la Memphis, is a dead giveaway to the shared cultural and historical roots of the two states. Black barbecue cooks, whose sauces and rubs tend to have slightly sweeter flavor profiles, have left their distinctive mark on barbecue in Texas, particularly in the big cities, just as they have in Memphis and Kansas City, where rural-to-urban migration resulted from a declining farm economy.

No matter who cooks it or what traditions it draws on, barbecue in Texas, as in most other barbecue cultures, is a social event, as well as a type of restaurant. Barbecue was—and is—the menu for political rallies, family celebrations, and community festivals. Whether for one hundred or for ten, barbecue is social.

Old-time Texas barbecue joints offered sliced brisket with sauce on the side and not much else. Traditionally, brisket was served in a faded plastic basket lined with paper or on a piece of butcher paper and placed unceremoniously on a wooden picnic table or a school desk. Eaten with fingers and slices of gooey white bread or saltines,

brisket frequently got a piquant garnish of sliced onion, pickled jalapeños, and dill pickle slices.

Some Hill Country spots still serve that way. Diners select the meat they want at the pit outside and take it inside on a tray, where it's weighed to price it. Then they sit at a plank table and eat barbecue off butcher paper with the traditional garnishes. Sauce comes on the side, as does coleslaw or beans. Cooper's in Mason and Junction and the Lone Star Barbecue in Brady—Hill Country towns—serve this way.

Now, more about that brisket. Pork barbecuers can't understand why anyone would work as hard as is necessary to get tender, juicy barbecued brisket. This stringy slab of meat is difficult to cook properly, while pork takes as naturally to smoke and coals as a good steak does to a big cabernet. But Texas is, after all, a beef state, and it is the heritage of barbecue everywhere that what goes on the pit is whatever doesn't taste good any other way. And brisket certainly qualifies.

Brisket comes from the chest/breast area of the animal and consists of alternating layers of muscle and fat. Try to select a brisket that is fairly uniform in size and thickness, although a brisket is always thicker at one end. A thick layer of fat is desirable because it will baste the meat while it cooks. Look for a brisket with thin, consistent streaks of marbling so there will be less visible fat in the cooked slices.

Since brisket is a notoriously tough cut of meat, selecting for tenderness may be impossible, but it can't hurt to try. Some experts say flexibility indicates a potential for tenderness. To test, lift a brisket from the center. The lower the ends droop, the more tender the brisket is likely to be.

Tenderness is what makes careful slicing a necessity. Even the best-prepared brisket won't be tender unless it is cut across the grain. Since the muscles in the brisket run in different directions, be prepared to turn the brisket and cut from a different direction as the grain changes. Begin by trimming off the layer of fat on top. Make thin slices from the pointed end, keeping in mind that midway you'll run into a thick layer of fat that separates the muscles. When you get there, check the grain and adjust the position of the brisket accordingly. If the meat tends to string instead of slice, you're no longer cutting across the grain. Save those pieces to use in chopped beef sandwiches. Reposition the brisket and try again.

Cooking with indirect heat is the main reason that brisket—with less fat marbled throughout than pork—can still be juicy and tender. Cooking brisket long enough to make it easy to slice without drying it out is the trick. To get good brisket, some tending is required, either to stoke the fire or to check the meat. But don't fuss with a brisket too much because every time you open the lid, you lose heat and smoke. Long, slow cooking at a constant low temperature produces good results.

Most Texas barbecue cooks season a brisket with a dry rub before cooking, although some prefer not to season with anything other than salt and pepper. Smoke does the rest of the flavoring. Some like to baste with a mop during smoking. Others think it's a waste of time and effort and simply adds to the cooking time.

LEGENDARY TEXAS BARBECUE RESTAURANTS

Angelo's
2533 White Settlement Rd., Fort Worth, TX 76107
Phone: 817-332-0357 (will ship barbecue)
Fax: 817-336-3091

Cooper's Barbecue
810 San Antonio (Hwy. 875), Mason, TX 76856 (about 2 hours west of Austin and San Antonio)
Phone: 915-347-6897 or 800-513-6963 (will ship barbecue)

Goode Co. Texas Barbecue
5109 Kirby Dr., Houston, TX 77098
Phone: 713-522-2530

Kreuz (say "Krites") Market
619 N. Colorado, Lockhart, TX 78644 (within 1 hour of Austin and San Antonio)
Phone: 512-398-2361
Fax: 512-376-5576

Lone Star Barbecue
210 S. Bridge, Brady, TX 76825 (about 2 hours west of Austin and San Antonio)
Phone: 915-597-1936 (will ship barbecue)
Fax: 915-591-2586
www.lonestarbbq.com

North Main BBQ (Fri.–Sun. only)
406 N. Main, Euless, TX 76039 (near
    DFW Airport, between Dallas and Fort
    Worth)
Phone: 817-283-0884
Fax: 817-684-8120

Railhead Smokehouse
2900 Montgomery St., Fort Worth, TX
    76107
Phone: 817-738-9808

The Salt Lick Barbecue Restaurant
18300 FM 1826, Driftwood, TX (within
    1 hour of Austin)
Phone: 512-858-4959
For shipping: 512-894-3117
www.saltlickbbq.com

Sonny Bryan's (multiple locations)
Original: 2202 Inwood Rd., Dallas, TX
    75235-7321
Phone: 214-357-7120

Texas Beef Brisket Barbecue

This is the real deal, the thing that distinguishes Texas barbecue from all the rest. Brisket, a big, flat, stringy piece of meat, can become fork tender and fine textured in a smoker. Here's how to do it.

Allow about 1 hour of cooking per pound of meat, plus a little more in case the fire gets too low or the meat's just tough and stubborn. And remember, brisket, like any other meat on the barbecue, takes longer to cook when the weather is cold.

Some cooks swear neither a rub nor a mop is necessary because the best brisket is simply flavored with salt and pepper and derives the rest of its flavor from the smoke. Suit yourself.

1 8- to 10-pound whole beef brisket, untrimmed (it should have a thick layer of fat on one side)

Texas Dry Rub (page 84) or salt and black pepper to taste

Texas Wet Mop (page 86), optional

Lone Star Barbecue Sauce (page 88), optional

10 to 12 white sandwich buns, optional

Dill pickle slices, sliced onions, and/or pickled jalapeño peppers, for garnish

1. Generously coat all sides of the brisket, particularly the fat layer, with the rub or salt and pepper. Cover and let the meat come to room temperature, about 1 hour.

2. Meanwhile, prepare a fire by lighting wood or a combination of wood and charcoal in the firebox of a cooker or at the end of a barrel smoker opposite the end with the vent or chimney. Or light the coals in a water smoker. Or preheat a gas smoker/grill.

3. When the fire has burned down to glowing embers or the coals are covered with gray ash, place the brisket on the grate but not directly over the coals. Or place a full pan of water over the coals or hot lava rocks, then add the grate and brisket. The fire should be low, 225° to 250°F.

4. Cover the cooker and smoke the brisket, turning every hour or so, until it is tender and the internal temperature reaches 180° to 190°F on an instant-read thermometer, 8 to 10 hours. Tend the fire by adding wood (or wood embers from a separate fire) or coals to keep it from going out and to keep the temperature inside the cooker between 225° and 300°F. If using a mop (basting is

advisable only when cooking without a water pan), brush it on when turning the brisket or after tending the fire.

5. When the brisket is charred and tender (a fork should insert easily), remove it from the cooker and allow to rest about 20 minutes.

6. Trim off the fat layer and cut brisket in thin slices across the grain. Serve with warm barbecue sauce, if desired. Or stack several slices in a sandwich bun spread lightly with sauce. Add more sauce, as desired.

7. Serve with pickles, sliced fresh onion rings, and jalapeño peppers.

Serves 10 to 12.

FAIL-SAFE TECHNIQUE: *The following technique produces smoky, tender brisket and cuts the time almost in half. Season the brisket as for long cooking. Light a fire in a charcoal grill that is big enough to hold the brisket. Allow the coals to burn until covered with gray ash. Place the brisket on the grill, fat side down. Grill the brisket about 45 minutes or until the fat is charred, turning when necessary to stop fat from dripping onto the fire. Squirt flare-ups with water to douse the flames. Remove the brisket from the grill.*

Preheat the oven to 250°F. Place the brisket on a double thickness of aluminum foil in a shallow roasting pan. Wrap it tightly and bake for 4 to 5 hours or until the meat is very tender. Remove the brisket from the oven and peel back the foil. Increase the oven temperature to 350°F. Return the brisket to the oven and roast, uncovered, for 30 minutes to crisp the top layer of fat. Allow the meat to rest for 20 minutes. Trim off the fat layer and cut across the grain into thin slices. Serve with barbecue sauce.

THE BASICS

TECHNIQUE: Indirect heat	**RUB:** Yes
SMOKE: Mesquite, oak, or hickory	**MOP:** Optional
TEMPERATURE: 225° to 300°F	**SAUCE:** On the side
TIME: 8 to 10 hours or as needed	

Chopped Barbecue Beef Sandwiches

Called "poor man's barbecue" because they're made from trimmings and bits of meat that fall away during slicing, chopped beef sandwiches are less expensive and a lot messier than sliced beef sandwiches. Some folks swear they're better! No matter which you prefer, chopped beef sandwiches are a great way to use up what's left after a big barbecue.

2 to 3 cups finely chopped Texas Beef Brisket Barbecue (page 75)	4 white sandwich buns
	½ cup chopped onion, optional
1 to 2 cups Lone Star Barbecue Sauce (page 88) or your choice of bottled sauce	½ cup dill pickle relish, optional

1. Place the chopped beef in a medium saucepan and add enough sauce to moisten. Heat over very low heat, stirring occasionally, until meat and sauce are hot.

2. Place the remaining sauce in a small saucepan and heat until bubbly; keep warm.

3. Assemble the sandwiches by placing ¼ to ½ cup of warmed meat with sauce on bottom half of sandwich bun. If desired, garnish with onion and relish. Or pass the onion and relish at the table.

4. Drizzle with additional sauce, if desired, or pass the sauce at the table.

Makes 4 sandwiches.

> *When you're cooking brisket, you have to be careful or you'll be making new soles for your boots.*
>
> —MICHAEL LEMASTER, PIT MASTER, SONNY BRYAN'S BARBECUE, DALLAS, TEXAS

Smoky Texas Ribs

Even in a beef state like Texas, pork spareribs are what you're eating when barbecued ribs are on the menu. Sometimes beef ribs, bigger and tougher, are available, but they'll be called beef ribs.

The most popular size of spareribs for barbecuing is called "three and down," meaning that a full thirteen-bone slab with chine bone and brisket flap weighs 3 pounds or less. Bigger ribs are too bony.

In Texas, as in Memphis, you can find proponents of wet and dry ribs, although Texas ribs tend toward the drier style. The flavor profile is the main distinction between Texas ribs and those elsewhere. Texas ribs are generally heavier on the spicy components, lighter on the sweet. And the wood is likely to be mesquite, at least in parts of the state where that rangy tree grows. Its smoke has a pungent aroma and produces a distinct flavor, different from the smoke of sweet woods. Arguments about style, flavor, and smoke ensue, but no one who smokes—and eats—a good rib ever really loses.

2 full racks of three-and-down pork spareribs (about 6 pounds)	Texas Wet Mop (page 86), optional
Texas Dry Rub (page 84)	Lone Star Barbecue Sauce (page 88)

1. To skin the ribs, use a blunt knife (even a screwdriver) to loosen the membrane and lift it from the bones. Once you get started, your fingers are the best tool for getting under the membrane to tear it away. Do this before seasoning the ribs with a rub or mop.

2. Coat the ribs generously with the rub. Press the spices into the meat with your fingers or the back of a spoon. Allow the ribs to come to room temperature, about 1 hour.

3. Prepare a fire by lighting wood or a combination of wood and charcoal in the firebox of a cooker or at the end of a barrel smoker opposite the end with the vent or chimney. Or light coals in a water smoker. Or preheat a gas smoker/grill.

4. When the fire has burned down to glowing embers or the coals are covered with gray ash, place the ribs, meaty side up, on the grate but not directly over the coals. Or place a full pan of water over the coals or hot lava rocks, then add the grate and ribs.

5. Cover the cooker and allow the ribs to smoke for 2 to 3 hours or until cooked through and tender. The temperature inside the cooker should be between 225° and 250°F. Add coals as needed to maintain it. If using the mop, baste the ribs on each side, turning and basting every 30 minutes. This will extend the cooking time by at least 1 hour.

6. The ribs should be browned and crisp on the exterior, tender on the inside. If desired, lightly brush one side of the ribs with the barbecue sauce and cook directly over the coals about 10 minutes to glaze them. Turn the ribs and lightly brush the other side. Cook directly over the coals about 10 minutes longer, just until the sauce sets and dries.

7. To serve, slice the ribs between the bones into individual pieces. Serve with additional barbecue sauce on the side.

Serves 4 to 6.

FAIL-SAFE TECHNIQUE: *Preheat the oven to 200°F. Place the seasoned ribs on baking sheets in the oven for 6 to 8 hours. This tenderizes and cooks them while setting the spices. During the last hour the ribs are in the oven, prepare a fire by lighting wood or a combination of wood and charcoal. Allow the coals to burn down to low or medium-low, with a heavy layer of ash. Lightly brush both sides of the ribs with sauce and cook over low coals on both sides until they are crisp and glazed, 20 to 30 minutes. Brush and turn the ribs several times while grilling, finishing with the meaty side up.*

TECHNIQUE: Indirect and direct heat	**RUB:** Yes
SMOKE: Mesquite, oak, or hickory	**MOP:** Optional
TEMPERATURE: 225° to 250°F	**SAUCE:** On the side or lightly basted on
TIME: 2 to 3 hours, up to 6 hours	during last 30 minutes

Barbecued Sausage

Sausage is a real typical go-with for barbecued brisket. It also makes a great appetizer, sliced and passed with toothpicks and sauce for dipping.

In barbecue shacks, plates are often sold with one, two, or three meats. Almost no one ever gets a plate with just sausage, but often it is the second or third choice on a combination platter. Use good-quality smoked (fully cooked) sausage of beef, turkey, pork, or venison (or a combination). Since you're basically heating the sausage over the coals, grilling takes only about 10 minutes. So serve it as an appetizer to hold off hunger pangs if the brisket isn't quite ready or save it for last and cook it while the brisket is resting.

2 links fully cooked smoked sausage (about 2 pounds)	1 cup (or more) Lone Star Barbecue Sauce (page 88) or your choice of bottled sauce

1. Place the whole links of sausage over low coals. Turn frequently with tongs (not a fork, or the juices will run and cause flare-ups) until heated through and the surface is browned and puffy.

2. Slice thin on the diagonal and serve with the sauce of your choice.

Serves 6 to 8.

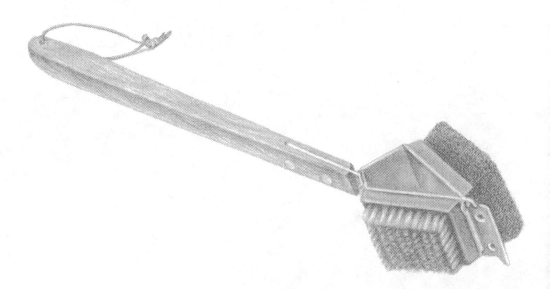

South Texas Cabrito

Cabrito is true South Texas/Hill Country barbecue, reflecting more Mexican than German influence. Junction, Texas, has one of the world's largest goat auctions, a testament to the number of Spanish goats raised in this part of the state. Each year the nearby town of Brady, in the geographical center of the state, holds a big goat cook-off.

The taste of cabrito (young goat) can be strong, so temper it with an acidic brine, then cook it long and slow. The addition of ginger to the rub helps tame the flavor, but the ultimate flavoring for goat is mesquite smoke. Even if you can't find mesquite wood, you can probably find mesquite chips, which can be added to the charcoal to provide the requisite flavor punch. Goat can be somewhat greasy and is often served as the second meat at a barbecue featuring brisket or ribs. If it seems like the recipe calls for a lot of meat, remember that the carcass has a high proportion of bone to meat, so cabrito doesn't provide all that much meat per pound.

Cabrito is often served with warm flour tortillas. The meat is wrapped in the tortilla along with fresh tomato salsa, called pico de gallo. Enjoy a bowl of beans on the side.

8 to 10 pounds baby goat

2 to 2½ gallons water

3 tablespoons salt

½ cup white vinegar

½ cup lemon juice

Rub for Cabrito (page 85)

Mop for Cabrito (page 87), optional

Lone Star Barbecue Sauce (page 88)

Salt, black pepper, and cayenne
    pepper to taste

2 to 3 fresh limes

2 to 3 dozen fresh flour tortillas, heated
    (see Tip, page 83)

Pico de Gallo (page 89) or your choice of
    bottled salsa

Cowboy Pinto Beans (page 138) or refried
    beans

1. Ask the butcher to cut the goat into manageable pieces (halves, quarters, or individual serving pieces), depending on the size of your cooker.

2. Rinse the pieces of cabrito. Combine the water, salt, vinegar, and lemon juice in a large tub or pot, stirring to dissolve the salt. If using fresh lemons, place the squeezed lemon halves along with goat pieces into the brine. Soak at least 1 hour or refrigerate overnight. Remove the goat from the brine and pat dry. Place it in a disposable aluminum roasting pan and season generously with the rub. Set aside while preparing the fire.

3. Prepare a fire by lighting mesquite wood or a combination of wood and charcoal in the firebox of a cooker or at the end of a barrel smoker opposite the end with the vent or chimney. Or light the coals in a water smoker. Or preheat a gas smoker/grill.

4. When the fire has burned down to glowing embers or the coals are covered with gray ash, place the roasting pan at the end of the smoker near the chimney, not directly over the coals. Or place a full pan of water over the coals or hot lava rocks, then position the grate and the roasting pan with cabrito.

5. Allow about 30 minutes per pound total cooking time. Tend the fire by adding wood (or wood embers from a separate fire) or coals to keep it from going out and to keep the temperature inside the cooker between 225° and 300°F. Turn the pieces occasionally for even cooking.

6. If using a mop, brush it on when turning the cabrito or after tending the fire. When the cabrito is tender, after 2 to 4 hours, remove the roasting pan from the cooker. Brush the cabrito with the barbecue sauce and place it directly over hot coals to glaze and crisp. Cook, turning occasionally and basting with additional sauce, 30 to 45 minutes longer, depending on the size of the pieces.

7. When the cabrito is crispy on the outside and tender inside, remove it from the fire and allow it to cool enough to handle. Wear heavy rubber gloves to handle the meat while it is hot.

8. Using your hands, pull the cabrito meat into shreds (like pulling barbecued pig), or chop the meat into small pieces. Reserve any drippings that accumulate while shredding or chopping. Pour the juices over the shredded cabrito. Season to taste with salt, pepper, cayenne pepper, and lime juice.

9. Serve with plenty of fresh flour tortillas, salsa, beans, and/or barbecue sauce. To make a cabrito burrito, spread refried beans in a thin layer on warm flour tortillas. Add several tablespoons of chopped cabrito meat to the middle of the tortilla. Garnish as desired with salsa and/or barbecue sauce. Fold and eat.

Serves 6 to 8.

FAIL-SAFE TECHNIQUE: *After removing the cabrito from the brine, season it with the rub. Preheat the oven to 325°F. Place the goat in a single layer in a large baking pan. Roast in the oven, uncovered, for about 1½ hours. Soak 1 to 2 cups (6 to 8 chunks) mesquite chips in enough water to cover while the meat is roasting. Meanwhile, prepare a fire. Place a layer of coals about 2 inches thick on the bottom of the grill. Pile coals into a pyramid and light. When the coals begin to glow red, spread them evenly over the bottom of the grill. This should take 30 to 45 minutes. Time your fire so that the coals are covered*

with gray ash when the goat comes out of the oven. The coals should be medium hot in intensity. You should be able to hold the palm of your hand close to (but, of course, not on) the cooking source for 5 to 6 seconds.

Remove the goat pieces from the oven and transfer to a platter or pan. Pour ½ cup drippings from the roasting pan into a measuring cup. Add an equal amount of water and stir. Take the roasted goat and drippings out to the grill.

Add soaked mesquite chips to the fire. Arrange the goat pieces evenly over the medium-hot coals. Baste with the diluted drippings. Cover and allow to cook for about 10 minutes. If there is considerable smoke, turn the pieces frequently to prevent burning. Continue grilling the cabrito, basting and turning frequently, for 30 to 45 minutes. During the last 15 minutes on the grill, brush the cabrito lightly with barbecue sauce. Grill until it is glazed. The outside should be brown and crispy, but not charred. Cool enough to handle. Follow the instructions above for shredding the meat and serving.

TIP: To heat flour tortillas, wrap them tightly in aluminum foil and place in a 300°F oven for 30 minutes or until they are hot. A microwave-safe tortilla warmer also works well. Follow the manufacturer's instructions or line the warmer with a paper towel lightly sprinkled with water. Place the tortillas in the warmer and cover with the lid. Microwave on high for 1 to 2 minutes or until the tortillas are hot.

THE BASICS

TECHNIQUE: Indirect and direct heat	RUB: Yes
SMOKE: Mesquite	MOP: Optional
TEMPERATURE: 225° to 300°F	SAUCE: Salsa and/or Lone Star Barbecue Sauce
TIME: 2 to 4 hours	

Texas Dry Rub

I n Texas rubs are more savory than they are sweet. Use this rub to season brisket before barbecuing. It's also good on ribs, steak, and chicken.

2 tablespoons salt	2 tablespoons paprika
2 tablespoons black pepper	2 tablespoons garlic powder

In an airtight container with a lid, combine the salt, pepper, paprika, and garlic powder. Shake to mix well. Sprinkle over the entire surface of the meat, concentrating on the fat layer. Rub or press into the fat and meat.

Makes $\frac{1}{2}$ cup.

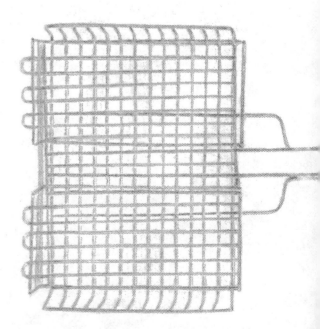

Rub for Cabrito

Ginger adds a beneficial touch to the seasoning blend for cabrito because it can moderate the gamy flavor of goat meat.

¼ cup garlic salt	1 tablespoon cayenne pepper
3 tablespoons ground ginger	

Combine the garlic salt, ginger, and cayenne pepper in a jar with a tight-fitting lid. Shake to mix. Lightly coat the surface of the cabrito before barbecuing.

Makes ½ cup.

Texans have taken a junk piece of meat and elevated it to an art form.

—CAROLYN WELLS, KANSAS CITY BARBECUE SOCIETY, KANSAS CITY, MISSOURI

Texas Wet Mop

Mops are sauces used during cooking but not at the table. Because they are used for basting, they don't contain any (or much) sugar, tomato sauce, or ketchup, which would cause them to burn.

1 teaspoon salt	1 large (or 2 small) bay leaf
1 teaspoon dry mustard	1 teaspoon red pepper sauce
1 teaspoon chili powder	1/2 cup Worcestershire sauce
2 teaspoons paprika	1/3 cup cider vinegar
1/3 cup vegetable oil	1 tablespoon soy sauce
2 cloves garlic, crushed	3 1/4 cups beef stock

1. In a medium saucepan, combine the salt, dry mustard, chili powder, paprika, and vegetable oil. Stir to make a paste. Add the remaining ingredients slowly, stirring all the while.

2. Place over medium heat and bring to a boil. Remove from the heat and allow to cool. Pour into a container with a tight-fitting lid and refrigerate until ready to use.

3. Brush the mop on beef or ribs while barbecuing over dry (no water pan), indirect heat.

Makes 1 quart.

Mop for Cabrito

1 cup (2 sticks) butter (or ½ cup butter and
    ½ cup bacon drippings)

¼ cup lime juice

1 tablespoon soy sauce

1 teaspoon salt

1 teaspoon black pepper

2 cloves garlic, crushed

1 teaspoon cayenne pepper

2 cups water

Combine all the ingredients in a medium saucepan. Bring to a boil over medium heat. Reduce the heat and simmer 5 minutes. Remove from the heat and allow to cool. Pour into a container with a tight-fitting lid and refrigerate to store, up to 2 weeks.

Makes about 3 cups.

Lone Star
Barbecue Sauce

This sauce is served at the table with sliced beef brisket, sausage, ribs, chicken, or cabrito. Don't baste with it. However, you can use it to glaze the barbecue during the last 20 minutes or so of cooking time.

For extra-smoky barbecue sauce, add some meat drippings. Obtain the drippings by placing a drip pan under the brisket during cooking or by saving the juices that collect while the meat rests and during slicing. You can also heat some of the fat trimmings to obtain some fat drippings.

1 1/4 cups ketchup	1/4 cup water
1/3 cup Worcestershire sauce	1 clove garlic, crushed
1/3 cup lemon juice	1/4 cup (1/2 stick) butter or pan drippings
1/3 cup packed brown sugar	from barbecue
1 tablespoon yellow mustard	

1. Combine the ketchup, Worcestershire sauce, lemon juice, brown sugar, mustard, water, and garlic in a medium saucepan. Place over very low heat and simmer, stirring occasionally, 1 hour. For really smoky flavor, place on the grill away from the heat source during the last hour of smoking.

2. Stir in the butter or drippings and cook 15 minutes longer. Pour into a container with a tight-fitting lid and refrigerate to store, up to 2 weeks.

Makes about 3 cups.

SHORTCUT: *Add meat drippings to bottled barbecue sauce for a sauce that tastes almost as good as home-made. Add 2 to 3 tablespoons barbecue pan drippings to 1 bottle barbecue sauce. Heat and serve.*

Pico de Gallo

Vine-ripened summer tomatoes are the best for this salsa, but hothouse tomatoes will do as long as they're bright red, sweet, and not at all grainy, like most supermarket tomatoes. Use fresh jalapeños, sweet onions, and cilantro for a true South Texas flavor. This salsa also enhances Cowboy Pinto Beans (page 138).

The heat factor in jalapeños can vary. If you don't want this relish too spicy, add them with care. And remember, wear rubber gloves to handle fresh peppers. Avoid touching your eyes, nose, or mouth after handling the peppers. Their juice can sting!

4 to 6 ripe tomatoes, coarsely chopped, to make 4 cups

1 large onion, coarsely chopped, to make 1½ cups

2 fresh jalapeño peppers, seeded and finely chopped, or to taste

1 teaspoon salt or to taste

¼ to ½ cup coarsely chopped fresh cilantro leaves or to taste

In a medium nonreactive bowl, combine the tomatoes, onion, and peppers. Stir in the salt and refrigerate about 1 hour. Stir in the cilantro just before serving. Taste and adjust the seasoning.

Makes about 5 cups.

Menu for Kansas City–Style Beef or Rib Barbecue Plate

Sliced brisket and/or ribs (pages 95 and 94)

S.H.T. Barbecue Sauce (page 102)

Barbecue Baked Beans (page 137)

Sweet-Sour Coleslaw (page 134) or Creamy Coleslaw (page 133)

Potato Salad with Mayonnaise and Hard-Cooked Eggs (page 141)

kansas city barbecue

where east meets west

Kansas City is the Constantinople of barbecue, where the pork tradition of the South meets head-on the beef tradition of Texas. Barbecue in Kansas City represents the best of both worlds. Both geographically and stylistically, Kansas City is the bridge between Texas and Southern barbecue styles.

Here brisket and ribs reign in happy harmony. KC brisket has obvious roots in Texas style, but ribs in Kansas City tend toward the wet: sweet, hot, and sticky. The controversy here—and there's got to be one if barbecue is involved—is over what makes good sauce. The variations are infinite.

KC barbecue devotees are passionate about sauce. For many, sauce is what separates good barbecue from great barbecue. Ironically, this style of thick, tomatoey sauce became the prototype for commercial sauce. Kraft brand, the world's first mass-produced and still best-selling barbecue sauce, is basically Kansas City style—tomatoey, sweet, and mildly spicy to appeal to the broadest number of palates. This is what most people think of as barbecue sauce.

It is no coincidence that one of America's most successful barbecue sauce barons, Dr. Rich Davis, hails from here. The physician pioneered the production of the excellent K.C. Masterpiece brand of barbecue sauce, which more accurately reflects the regional character. If you want an example of sweet-tangy Kansas City–style sauce, try a bottle. It is widely available.

Despite the common denominators, there are almost as many sauce variations as there are Kansas City barbecue cooks. Just ask cook-off champion Paul Kirk, who travels from coast to coast giving barbecue lessons. He's made a study of rubs and sauces and will tell you that no place is more fascinated by sauce, all kinds of sauce, than Kansas City.

In his classes, however, the self-styled Baron of Barbecue maintains that it is the seasoning on the meat that establishes the flavor profile for barbecue. Kirk advises that balance, primarily between salt and sugar, is the key to a successful rub. That applies to the aggregate amounts, i.e., the total amount of salt—table salt, hickory salt, and garlic salt, for example—and the total amount of sugars, whether white, brown, maple, or a combination. Paprika is the next prominent ingredient in the Kirk rub formula, making up a third to half the amount of salt and sugar. It gives the rub color, as well as some sweet-hot notes. The rest of the formula is pretty free-form, including chili powder or black pepper and touches of other ingredients like cayenne, cumin, cinnamon, and allspice.

Good sauce, says Kirk, seasons and enhances; it doesn't overpower or hide the flavor of barbecue. The typical Kansas City–style sauce is thick, with a tomato base, and contains notes of sweetness, sour tang, and spices. It has enough body to be brushed on meats toward the end of cooking as a "finishing sauce" and to be served at the table as a garnish.

In good Midwestern tradition, Kansas City barbecue blends elements from all the barbecue regions, but it isn't all melting pot. There's a unique tradition known as "burnt ends" or "burnt edges." Whether from the ends or the flap of the brisket, "ends" and "edges" are the crispy, charred, fatty pieces—elsewhere known as trimmings.

When in Kansas City, ask for burnt ends or edges. The person taking your order will know what you're talking about, although the menu will probably list them as well. But you won't always get an order because they sell out fast. Some restaurants resort to charring extra pieces so they'll have "faux ends" to satisfy demand.

Kansas City's spot on the map accounts for its blending of barbecue cultures. As a rail center in the middle of the country (along with sister city St. Louis), the city was a major destination for Texas cattle on their journey from trail to table. The beef brisket tradition came with the bovines.

Southern traditions are strong here too. After all, Missouri—though deep in the heart of the Midwest—is neighbored by Kentucky and Tennessee. Memphis is just a ways east and downriver on the mighty Mississippi, so the flavors and customs of Memphis barbecue have strongly influenced Kansas City style.

Some barbecue lovers, particularly those from St. Louis, lay claim to a St. Louis style. That city's namesake contribution to barbecue is the term St. Louis cut, which refers to a particular size (3 pounds or less) and butchering technique for a slab of spareribs, the classic ribs for barbecue.

Spareribs—the lower section of the

ribcage remaining after the pork chop has been removed—are said to be cut St. Louis style when the chine and brisket bones are trimmed from the bottom of the rib rack. Since those particular bones are mostly waste, their removal makes St. Louis–cut ribs more expensive but worth the price. The meat should be moist, pink, and not too fatty. Kansas City–cut ribs are similar but trimmed even more than the St. Louis cut.

Still another major influence on Kansas City barbecue is its celebrated black barbecue cooks, some widely known and others heroes just in their immediate neighborhood. Like nearby Memphis, Kansas City was a major destination for rural African-Americans, and there's the same visceral connection between barbecue and jazz in this city as in Memphis. Black cooks brought their expertise to town and established some of the city's best-known barbecue restaurants. The most renowned is Arthu Bryant's, proclaimed by Kansas City writer Calvin Trillin to be "the world's best restaurant."

Nowhere are there more barbecue zealots than in Kansas City. For many here, barbecue isn't just a business or a backyard pasttime. It is a lifestyle, especially for those who travel the country competing. One of the nation's major sanctioning organizations, the Kansas City Barbecue Society, calls this city home. With evangelistic zeal, the KCBS spreads the word about the superb merits of barbecue. It is the sanctioning organization and rule maker for contests all over the country at which barbecue cooks try to accumulate enough points to compete in the world series of bar-

becue, the American Royal Barbecue, held here in October.

LEGENDARY KANSAS CITY BARBECUE RESTAURANTS

Amazing Grace's Bar-B-Q
3832 Main St., Kansas City, MO 64111
Phone: 816-531-7557
Fax: 816-531-8946
www.grandemporium.com

Arthur Bryant's
1727 Brooklyn, Kansas City, MO 64127
Phone: 816-231-1123 (will ship barbecue)

Fiorella's Jack Stack Barbecue (multiple locations)
13441 Holmes, Martin City, KS 65145
Phone: 877-419-7427 (will ship barbecue)
Fax: 816-452-1176
www.jackstackbbq.com

Gates & Sons (multiple locations)
Headquarters, 4621 Paseo, Kansas City, MO 64110
Phone: 816-923-0900 or 800-662-7427 (RIBS) to order sauce and seasonings
Fax: 816-923-3922
www.gatesbbq.com

K.C. Masterpiece Barbecue & Grill (multiple locations)
10985 Metcalf, Overland Park, KS 66210
Phone: 913-345-1199
www.ksmrestaurants.com

Kansas City–Style Sticky Ribs

Ribs are what really set barbecue-loving hearts aflutter in Kansas City. While brisket is a staple, ribs are the pièce de résistance.

2 full racks of three-and-down pork spareribs (about 6 pounds)	1 cup (2 sticks) melted margarine, optional
KC Sweet and Hot Rub (page 99)	KC Sweet and Hot Sauce (page 101)

1. To skin the ribs, use a blunt knife (even a screwdriver) to loosen the membrane and lift it from the bones. Once you get started, your fingers are the best tool for getting under the membrane to tear it away. Do this before seasoning the ribs with a rub or mop.

2. Coat the ribs generously with the rub. Press the spices into the meat with your fingers or the back of a spoon. Let the ribs come to room temperature, about 1 hour.

3. Meanwhile, prepare a fire by lighting wood or a combination of wood and charcoal in the firebox of a cooker or at the end of a barrel smoker opposite the end with the vent or chimney. Or light the coals in a water smoker. Or preheat a gas smoker/grill.

4. When the fire has burned down to glowing embers or the coals are covered with gray ash, place the ribs, meaty side up, on the grate but not directly over the coals. Or place a full pan of water over the coals or hot lava rocks, then add the grate and ribs.

5. Cover the cooker and allow the ribs to smoke for 2 to 3 hours or until cooked through and tender. The temperature inside the cooker should be between 225° and 250°F. Add coals as needed to maintain it. After the first 30 minutes, baste the ribs lightly on all sides with the melted margarine, if desired. Repeat every 30 minutes or so until the ribs are browned. Brush the ribs generously on all sides with the barbecue sauce and cook over low, direct heat 30 minutes longer to glaze.

6. To serve, slice the ribs between the bones into individual pieces.

Serves about 6.

FAIL-SAFE TECHNIQUE: *Preheat the oven to 200°F. Place the seasoned ribs on baking sheets in the oven for about 3 hours. This tenderizes and cooks them while setting the spices. The ribs won't brown at this temperature; that's OK. During the last hour the ribs are in the oven, prepare a fire by lighting wood or a combination of wood and charcoal. Allow the coals to burn down to low or medium-low, with a heavy layer of ash. Place the ribs directly over the low coals and cook until browned, turning occasionally to cook evenly.*

When the ribs are browned, after about 20 minutes, brush both sides with sauce and cook, meaty side up, about 15 minutes longer.

TIP: For extra-sticky, falling-off-the-bone-tender KC-style ribs, mop the ribs with melted margarine while smoking. After smoking the ribs for 1½ to 2 hours, brush them with honey, if desired, wrap tightly in aluminum foil, and let stand for 1 hour. This adds succulent flavor and steam-tenderizes the ribs. Unwrap and return the ribs to the coals for about 30 minutes, brushing them generously with sauce several times, until they are glazed and heavily coated with sauce.

For super tender ribs, remove the glazed ribs from the grill and immediately transfer them to foil. Wrap tightly and let stand for 1 hour longer. Keep warm. (This tip is courtesy of Karen Putman, head grill madam of the Kansas City Que Queens competition cooking team.)

TECHNIQUE: Indirect and direct heat	**RUB:** Yes
SMOKE: Hickory, pecan, or apple	**MOP:** Optional
TEMPERATURE: 225° to 250°F	**SAUCE:** Yes
TIME: 2 to 3 hours	

KC-Style Barbecued Brisket

The flavor profile of this beef is classic Kansas City, sweet and tangy instead of peppery-savory, à la Texas. Making tough, stringy brisket turn out juicy and tender is a true art. (See the guidelines for selecting brisket on pages 72–73.)

1 8- to 10-pound whole beef brisket, untrimmed (it should have a thick layer of fat on one side)	Show-Me-State Wet Mop (page 99), optional
KC Sweet and Hot Rub (page 99)	KC Sweet and Hot Sauce (page 101), optional

1. Generously coat all sides of the brisket, particularly the fat layer, with the rub. Cover and let the meat come to room temperature, about 1 hour.

2. Meanwhile, prepare a fire by lighting wood or a combination of wood and charcoal in the firebox of a cooker or at the end of a barrel smoker opposite the end with the vent or chimney. Or light the coals in a water smoker. Or preheat a gas smoker/grill.

3. When the fire has burned down to glowing embers or the coals are covered with gray ash, place the brisket on the grate but not directly over the coals. Or place a full pan of water over the coals or hot lava rocks, then add the grate and brisket. The fire should be low, 225° to 250°F.

4. Cover the cooker and smoke the brisket, turning every hour or so, until it is tender and the internal temperature reaches 180° to 190°F on an instant-read thermometer, 8 to 10 hours.

5. Tend the fire by adding wood (or wood embers from a separate fire) or coals to keep it from going out and to keep the temperature inside the cooker between 225° and 300°F. If using a mop (basting is advisable only when cooking without a water pan), brush it on when turning the brisket or after tending the fire.

6. When the brisket is charred and tender (a fork should insert easily), remove it from the cooker and allow to rest about 20 minutes.

7. Trim off the fat layer and cut the brisket into thin slices across the grain. (See the guidelines for slicing brisket on page 73.) Serve with warm barbecue sauce, if desired.

Serves 10 to 12.

FAIL-SAFE TECHNIQUE: *The following technique produces smoky, tender brisket and cuts the time almost in half. Season the brisket as for long cooking. Light a fire in a charcoal grill that is big enough to hold the brisket. Allow the coals to burn until covered with ash. Place the brisket on the grill, fat side down. Grill the brisket about 45 minutes or until the fat is charred, turning when necessary to stop fat from dripping onto the fire. Squirt flare-ups with water to douse the flames. Remove the brisket from the grill.*

Preheat the oven to 250°F. Place the brisket on a double thickness of aluminum foil in a shallow roasting pan. Wrap it tightly and bake for 4 to 5 hours or until the meat is very tender. Remove the brisket from the oven and peel back the foil. Increase the temperature to 350°F. Return the brisket to the oven and roast, uncovered, for 30 minutes to crisp the top layer of fat. Allow the meat to rest for 20 minutes. Trim off the fat layer and cut across the grain into thin slices. Serve with barbecue sauce.

THE BASICS

TECHNIQUE: Indirect heat	RUB: Yes
SMOKE: Hickory, pecan, or apple	MOP: Optional
TEMPERATURE: 225° to 300°F	SAUCE: Optional
TIME: 8 to 10 hours	

KC Burnt Edges

Beware of high-volume barbecue restaurants that sell "burnt edges." True burnt edges or burnt ends—the charred, crispy, dry edges that are trimmed from the brisket before slicing—are hard to come by. That's simply because even a big brisket produces a relatively small amount of trimmings other than the layer of fat on top. Discard most of the fat, saving a few small pieces to flavor beans and sauces.

Often what is sold as burnt edges is just chopped, charred brisket or meat that has been soaked in barbecue sauce. Burnt edges are served between slices of soft white bread or in a sandwich bun.

1 KC-Style Barbecued Brisket (page 95)

1½ to 2 cups KC Sweet and Hot Sauce (page 101) or your choice of bottled sauce

4 to 6 soft white sandwich buns

1. After removing the brisket from the cooker, trim off the fat layer and discard the fat. Trim off and save the edges of the brisket, particularly areas that seem charred crisp or dry. Finely chop the crisp edges and slice the brisket.

2. Select the less uniform slices and finely chop enough to make 4 cups when combined with the chopped trimmings. Add enough sauce to make a spoonable sandwich filling, similar in consistency to Sloppy Joes.

3. Serve the edges in soft white sandwich buns.

Serves 4 to 6.

What you grew up with is what you like.

—CAROLYN WELLS, KANSAS CITY BARBECUE SOCIETY,
KANSAS CITY, MISSOURI

Paul Kirk's Basic Barbecue Rub

Paul Kirk teaches this basic rub formula to his barbecue classes, encouraging his students to customize it to their own taste. He recommends this as an all-purpose rub for beef, lamb, pork, chicken, or fish. Apply liberally.

1 cup sugar	2 tablespoons black pepper
¼ cup seasoned salt	1 tablespoon lemon pepper
¼ cup garlic salt	2 teaspoons ground sage
¼ cup celery salt	1 teaspoon dry mustard
¼ cup onion salt	½ teaspoon ground thyme
½ cup paprika	½ teaspoon cayenne pepper
3 tablespoons chili powder	

Combine all the ingredients in a sifter and sift to blend well. Store in an airtight jar in the refrigerator. The rub keeps, refrigerated, for 2 to 3 weeks; frozen, for 6 months.

Makes about 3 cups.

Dry spices are more consistent than fresh.

—PAUL KIRK, SEVEN-TIME WORLD CHAMPION BARBECUE COOK AND BARBECUE TEACHER, KANSAS CITY, MISSOURI

KC Sweet and Hot Rub

This seasoning blend has the sweet-hot flavor for which KC is famous. Cayenne pepper adds a potent burn. Use it in moderation until you find a comfortable, but slightly challenging, heat level.

¼ cup paprika	1 tablespoon garlic powder
¼ cup sugar	2 to 3 teaspoons cayenne pepper or to taste, optional
2 tablespoons salt	
2 tablespoons black pepper	

In an airtight container with a lid, combine all the ingredients. Shake to mix well.

Makes about 1 cup.

Show-Me-State Wet Mop

Try using this mop as a marinade for brisket prior to cooking. Set aside 1 cup to use later as a mop. Pour the remainder over the brisket. Marinate for 4 to 6 hours, refrigerated. When ready to cook, remove the meat from the marinade and pat dry. Season with a rub.

To use the mop as a basting sauce during smoking, paint it on the brisket every 30 minutes or so, starting about halfway through the cooking process.

3 cups beef stock	2 teaspoons seasoned salt
¾ cup Worcestershire sauce	1 teaspoon granulated onion
1 tablespoon chili powder	1 teaspoon granulated garlic
1 teaspoon celery salt	¾ cup lemon juice

Combine all the ingredients except the lemon juice in a nonreactive saucepan. Bring to a boil, lower the heat, and simmer about 15 minutes, stirring occasionally. Stir in the lemon juice and let cool. The mixture should be slightly warm but not hot enough to cook the meat.

Makes about 4 cups.

Paul Kirk's Kansas City Barbecue Sauce

Here's the formula for a totem sauce from the sauce capital of the barbecue world. An old-style recipe, it starts with butter, and plenty of it. Brush it on chicken or pork ribs about 30 minutes before the end of cooking time. At the table, serve it warm or chilled with chicken, pork ribs, or sliced beef brisket.

CELEBRATING

BARBECUE

100

½ cup (1 stick) butter

4 cloves garlic, pressed

1 cup minced onions

1 lemon, seeded and minced, including peel

1 32-ounce bottle ketchup

1 cup tomato juice

1 cup V-8 juice

1 cup packed brown sugar

½ cup molasses

½ cup Worcestershire sauce

¼ cup chili powder

¼ cup white vinegar

2 tablespoons black pepper

1 teaspoon salt

Melt the butter in a nonreactive saucepan over medium heat. Add the garlic, onions, and lemon. Cook until the onion is tender but not browned, about 4 minutes. Add the remaining ingredients. Bring the mixture to a boil, lower the heat, and simmer, stirring occasionally, for 1 to 1½ hours or until the sauce has thickened. Store, refrigerated, for up to 2 weeks.

Makes about 8 cups.

KC Sweet and Hot Sauce

This is a good—i.e., typically sweet, hot, and sticky—Kansas City-style table sauce. Brush it on ribs during the last 30 minutes of cooking. At the table, serve it warm with sliced brisket and/or ribs.

If you're in a hurry, you can add meat drippings to bottled barbecue sauce for a sauce that tastes almost as good as homemade.

2 cups ketchup	½ cup cider vinegar
½ cup packed dark brown sugar	1 clove garlic, mashed
1 tablespoon paprika	¼ cup chili sauce
2 to 3 teaspoons red pepper sauce	1 to 2 teaspoons salt or to taste
½ cup (1 stick) butter	

Combine the ingredients in a small saucepan over low heat. Stir and cook until the sugar and butter melt and the sauce is well blended. Simmer, stirring frequently to prevent sticking and burning, about 20 minutes. Store refrigerated, up to 2 weeks.

Makes about 3½ cups.

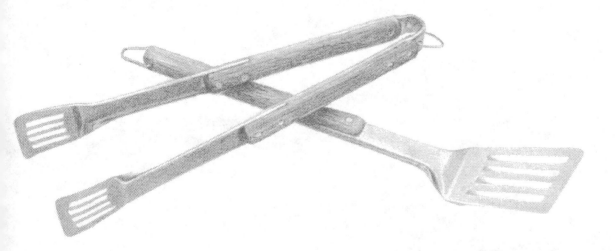

S.H.T. Barbecue Sauce

An even sweeter, hotter, and thicker sauce. Brush it on ribs during the last 30 minutes of cooking. At the table, serve it warm with sliced brisket and/or ribs.

1¼ cups bottled chili sauce	1 to 2 teaspoons red pepper sauce or to taste, optional
1½ cups ketchup	1 to 2 teaspoons lemon juice or to taste
½ cup packed brown sugar	1 teaspoon salt or to taste
1 cup root beer	
¼ cup (½ stick) butter	
2 to 3 tablespoons Worcestershire sauce or to taste	

Combine all the ingredients in a small saucepan over low heat. Stir and cook until the sugar and butter melt and the sauce is well blended. Simmer, stirring frequently to prevent sticking and burning, about 20 minutes.

Makes about 4 cups.

wild cards

*santa maria beef barbecue, owensboro
mutton barbecue, st. louis barbecued
snouts, and playing chicken*

This chapter takes a look at some of the micro-styles, as well as the universal elements that make barbecue so interesting.

While the four major styles of barbecue can be found to varying degrees all over the United States, some styles are so specialized they haven't spread far from their place of origin. A couple that are widely documented and recognized by barbecue aficionados are the Santa Maria, California, rancho style and the Owensboro, Kentucky, technique for cooking mutton or lamb. And then there are snouts, pronounced "snoots." Grilled pig faces. They're a delicacy in St. Louis, Missouri.

If snouts are a micro-regionalism, then chicken is the national barbecue. Just about every barbecue culture enjoys chicken slow-cooked over smoking coals. The tastes may vary from region to region, but as long as it tastes good, chicken isn't something barbecue advocates declare war over.

From the Santa Maria Valley in central California, the rancho style of barbecue draws on the traditions of Spanish rancheros. So specific are the cut of meat, the seasonings, the wood, the method of cooking, and the menu that the city of Santa Maria restricts the use of its name through copyright law.

Here's the deal: A cut of top sirloin, known as a tri-tip roast, is seasoned with salt, black pepper, and garlic salt. It is grilled over red oak, sliced, and served immediately with pinquito beans (a small red bean similar to a pinto but grown only in the area), macaroni and cheese, tossed green salad, toasted french bread, and Santa Maria salsa.

Kathy Murphy, an authorized Santa Maria caterer and foreman of Ranch Hands Barbeque Catering, Inc., says the tri-tip is easy to find in California supermarkets but concedes it is harder to come by in other parts of the country. Nevertheless, she says, a knowledgeable butcher can cut the triangular-shaped muscle.

So if you want to do Santa Maria, you should go to the trouble to find a tri-tip, Murphy advises. No other cut has the right texture, shape, and thickness to produce the same flavor and varying degrees of doneness in the prescribed 45 minutes cooking time. The edges should be medium to medium-well, and the interior medium with just a little pink. Slices are served in a big pan so that diners can pick their desired degree of doneness.

This tradition grew out of the cheap lunches prepared for mostly Hispanic farm and ranch workers using a fairly tough, less desirable cut of beef. Now, *that's* a familiar theme when it comes to the origins of just about all barbecue.

Kentucky has a localized barbecue tradition of its own: mutton à la Owensboro, in the western part of the state. The tariff of

1816 encouraged wool production in what was then the western frontier. That meant farmers raised lots of sheep. When the sheep got too old to produce top-quality wool, their next best use was as barbecue. They were cooked very much the same way pigs were cooked in the Carolinas.

The Moonlite B-B-Q Inn in Owensboro still serves a traditional mutton (that's a mature animal of two years, as opposed to a lamb or yearling) with a strong taste. At the diner large pieces of mutton are cooked with a vinegar mop for 12 hours directly over low coals.

Barbecued snouts come from East St. Louis, the part of town where all the packing houses once were located. Throw-away parts like snouts and the surrounding facial tissue became delicacies in the hands of the economically deprived but culinarily rich African-Americans in the nearby neighborhoods. Although most of the packing houses are now gone, the barbecue tradition in general, and snouts in particular, remains strong in this city on the Mississippi River. Snouts are a decidedly local tradition, one that St. Louis barbecue lovers nurture to this day.

The texture of a barbecued snout is similar to that of cracklings or chicharróns (pork rinds rendered by frying): crunchy on the outside, somewhat greasy on the inside. They're cooked slowly directly over low coals (sometimes indirectly to prevent burning) until the fat is rendered. Then they are dipped in barbecue sauce, returned to the grill directly over the coals to glaze them, and served between two pieces of white bread. A decidedly acquired taste, snouts (which include the nose) can be specially ordered by the case from a meat wholesaler (see Sources of Ingredients, page 172), although a trip to St. Louis might be less involved.

Every barbecue culture enjoys a barbecued bird, and there are as many versions as there are cooks. In fact, most of the rubs and sauces in this book will work just fine on chicken. Be careful if you're thinking of using a mop. Chicken burns easily when the fat drips on the coals. Adding a mop or marinade encourages the coals to flare and makes it more difficult to maintain a low, even temperature for thorough cooking. And no one likes pink, medium-rare chicken meat.

In the interest of providing a full range of recipes, this chapter also includes a recipe for barbecued whole fish.

SOME RESTAURANTS THAT SERVE BARBECUE SPECIALTIES

SANTA MARIA BEEF BARBECUE

Far Western Tavern
899 Guadalupe St., Guadalupe, CA 93434
Phone: 805-343-2211

The Hitching Post
3325 Point Sal Rd., Casmalia, CA
93429
Phone: 805-937-6151

El Rancho
2886 Mission Dr. (Route 246), Solvang, CA
93463
Phone: 805-688-4300

OWENSBORO MUTTON BARBECUE

The Moonlite B-B-Q Inn
2840 W. Parrish Ave., Owensboro, KY
42301
Phone: 270-684-8143 (will ship
barbecue)
www.moonlite.com
Email: janbbq@aol.com

ST. LOUIS BARBECUED SNOUTS

C&K Barbecue
4390 Jennings Sta. Rd., St. Louis, MO
63121
Phone: 314-385-8100
Fax: 314-385-8492
www.ckbarbecue.com

Santa Maria Barbecue

Strictly speaking, Santa Maria–style barbecue isn't true barbecue. The meat is grilled at too high a temperature and is ready when it is a lovely medium to medium-rare, pink and juicy in the middle, instead of well-done. Still, this ranch style is a noble tradition with an interesting history and makes a beautiful plate. Slice it thin and serve it with the prescribed menu:

Santa Maria Salsa (page 126)
Santa Maria–Style Pinquito Beans (page 139)
Macaroni and Cheese (page 147)
Leafy Greens, Pears, and Pecans with Sherry Vinaigrette (page 135)
    or your choice of tossed green salad

The recipes—with some adaptations—are from the Santa Maria Chamber of Commerce, courtesy of Santa Maria caterer Kathy Murphy.

1 3-pound tri-tip roast	Salt, black pepper, and garlic salt to taste

1. An hour before cooking, remove the meat from the refrigerator. Generously season it on all sides with salt, pepper, and garlic salt.

2. Prepare a fire by lighting oak wood (preferably Santa Maria Valley red oak, if available) or a combination of any wood and charcoal in the firebox of a cooker or at the end of a barrel smoker opposite the end with the vent or chimney. Or preheat one side of a gas smoker/grill. The fire should be medium-high, 350° to 375°F.

3. Place the meat directly over the coals and brown it on all sides. Cover the cooker while the meat browns but check frequently to prevent charring.

4. When the meat is browned, move it to a cooler portion of the grill, ideally 300° to 325°F. Turn and cook as needed to produce a medium (pink, not red) center in 45 minutes' cooking time.

5. Remove the meat from the grill and allow it to rest 15 minutes, loosely tented with foil. Slice thin, reserving any juices that accumulate, and serve immediately. Pour the juices over the meat just before serving.

Serves 8 to 10.

FAIL-SAFE TECHNIQUE: *If the fire gets too hot and the meat seems to be cooking too fast after browning on all sides, place it in a preheated 325°F oven and roast to the desired degree of doneness. It should register 140° to 145°F internal temperature on an instant-read meat thermometer.*

TIP: *Can't find a tri-tip? Grill a thick (3-inch) piece of sirloin, seasoned according to Santa Maria tradition.*

TECHNIQUE: Direct and indirect heat	**TIME:** 45 minutes to 1 hour
SMOKE: California red oak or other oak	**RUB:** Yes
TEMPERATURE: 350° to 375°F; 300° to 325°F	**MOP:** No
	SAUCE: No

Owensboro-Style Barbecued Lamb Shoulder

Since true mutton is difficult (if not impossible) for most home cooks to obtain, the following recipe uses a lamb shoulder roast, preferably 7 to 8 pounds. Even that will probably require a custom order from a butcher.

It is possible to use a leg of lamb (bone-in or butterflied) and reduce the cooking time, but this technique is designed for something tougher and more strongly flavored than leg of lamb, which is best served medium-rare instead of well-done and falling off the bone.

Although Kentucky tradition is to cook mutton over direct heat, this recipe also works well in a smoker; there is less chance of overcooking the meat. Serve it with this typical sauce, almost as black as night.

1 7- to 8-pound lamb shoulder roast

½ cup Worcestershire sauce or as needed

Owensboro-Style Barbecue Rub
   (page 119)

Owensboro-Style Barbecue Mop
   (page 120)

Owensboro-Style Black Barbecue Dip
   (page 122)

1. Rinse and dry the lamb shoulder. Coat the meat with Worcestershire sauce. Sprinkle the rub over the lamb, patting to help it adhere. Place the meat in a plastic bag and refrigerate several hours or overnight.

2. An hour before cooking, remove the meat from the refrigerator and allow to come to room temperature.

3. Meanwhile, prepare a fire by lighting wood or a combination of wood and charcoal in the firebox of a cooker or at the end of a barrel smoker opposite the end with the vent or chimney. Or light the coals in a water smoker. Or preheat a gas smoker/grill.

4. When the fire has burned down to glowing embers or the coals are covered with gray ash, place the lamb, fat side up, on the grate but not directly over the coals. Or place a full pan of water over the coals or hot lava rocks, then add the grate and lamb. The fire should be low, 225° to 250°F.

5. Cover the cooker. After the first hour of cooking, baste with the mop about once an hour until the meat is done. Allow 1 to 1½ hours per pound, or 7 to 10 hours. Tend the fire by adding wood or charcoal (or hot coals from a separate fire) to keep it from going out and to keep the temperature in-

side the cooker between 225° and 250°F. The meat should be well-done and tender, with an internal temperature that registers 180° to 190°F on an instant-read thermometer.

6. Slice the meat or shred and chop it as for Carolina pulled pork. Serve with the sauce (dip) on a plate or in a sandwich.

Serves 6 to 8.

FAIL-SAFE TECHNIQUE: *If the lamb looks too dry (or you start to think it will never get done), preheat the oven to 325°F. Remove the lamb to a shallow roasting pan. Roast 1 hour. Test for doneness with an instant-read thermometer; the internal temperature should be 180° to 190°F.*

TECHNIQUE: Direct or indirect heat	**TIME:** 7 to 10 hours
SMOKE: Hickory, oak, pecan, or other sweet wood	**RUB:** Yes
	MOP: Yes
TEMPERATURE: 225° to 250°F	**SAUCE:** Yes

Burgoo

This is the Kentucky equivalent of Brunswick stew, except it is even thicker and richer, thanks to the addition of beef and pork. Burgoo is often served with barbecue in the Kentucky part of the smoked-meat universe.

1 2½- to 3-pound chicken	¼ cup minced fresh parsley
2 pounds oxtail or beef shank	1 14½-ounce can crushed tomatoes
1 pound boneless pork, such as shoulder or fresh ham	1 8-ounce package frozen baby lima beans
2 teaspoons salt	½ cup chopped green pepper
1 teaspoon black pepper	2 cloves garlic, crushed
¼ teaspoon cayenne pepper	1 8-ounce package frozen whole-kernel corn
2 medium potatoes, peeled and cubed	
1 small onion, chopped	1 tablespoon Worcestershire sauce
½ cup peeled and chopped carrots	1 teaspoon red pepper sauce or to taste

1. Rinse the chicken inside and out; drain. Place the chicken, oxtail, and pork in a large stewpot or Dutch oven with water to cover. Add the salt and the black and cayenne peppers. Over high heat, bring the liquid to a boil. Reduce the heat, cover, and simmer 1½ to 2 hours or until the meats are very tender.

2. Remove the meats from the broth and cool enough to handle. Discard the chicken skin and bones. Separate the beef from the bones. Chop or shred the chicken, beef, and pork and return them to the broth.

3. Add the potatoes, onion, carrots, parsley, tomatoes with their juice, lima beans, green pepper, and garlic. Over high heat, bring the liquid to a boil. Reduce the heat, cover, and simmer 1 hour, stirring occasionally. Add the corn and simmer 20 to 30 minutes longer. Add the Worcestershire sauce. Taste and adjust the seasoning with more salt and pepper, if desired. Add red pepper sauce to taste. Burgoo should be spicy but not hot.

Serves 6 to 8.

St. Louis Barbecued Snouts

One of the liveliest barbecue books, *Smokestack Lightning: Adventures in the Heart of Barbecue Country*, by Lois Eric Elie, presents an astonishingly rich and authentic glimpse of the St. Louis barbecued snout tradition. Although the book doesn't give a recipe, it describes the process. That, plus a couple of barbecue fans who grew up in St. Louis loving snouts, helped create the following formula.

Once you get past the idea, the reality is an intriguing mix of grease, sweet, hot, acid, and tang—not altogether pleasant but certainly not as challenging as chitterlings. If you're ever in St. Louis, seek out a restaurant that serves snouts.

A hog snout consists of facial skin and nostrils—a little bit of muscle meat and a lot of fat. About the size of a salad plate, a snout goes onto the grill without seasoning. Only after as much fat as possible is rendered and the skin is crisp can a snout be declared ready to eat. Then pieces of snout go between a couple of slices of white bread slathered with barbecue sauce. Expect the skin side to be very chewy, almost like a canine toy made from hide.

10 hog snouts or more as desired	20 slices of white bread or 2 per snout,
St. Louis Barbecue Sauce (page 123)	or more

1. Rinse and dry the snouts. Trim off the excess fat, i.e., the ragged pieces or big globs. Find the big white tendons; remove and discard. Score the fat side of the snout to prevent curling.

2. Meanwhile, prepare a fire. Use enough coals to spread in a single layer over half of the bottom of the cooker. Pile together and light the coals. When they are covered with gray ash, spread them evenly over half of the bottom of the cooker.

3. When the fire is ready, place the snouts, meat side down, directly over the coals. Cover with the lid and cook 10 to 15 minutes. If the snouts begin to get too dark or appear charred, move them away from the hot coals. Keep adding coals to maintain a steady, glowing bed.

4. Turn the snouts. Continue checking and repositioning them until most of the fat is rendered. You'll know because there won't be as much sizzle coming from the cooker. Try not to turn the snouts more than two or three times. The total cooking time should be 2 to 2½ hours, but don't rely on time; rely on appearance. They should be crisp and crackly on the exterior, charred in places, and deep golden brown in color.

5. When the snouts are golden and crisp, brush them all over with barbecue sauce and reposi-

tion them directly over the coals. Cook, turning once or twice, until the sauce is cooked in and the surface is glazed, 10 to 15 minutes. Do not allow to burn.

6. Remove the snouts from the grill. Using shears, cut them into pieces about the size of a slice of bread or into strips. Slather a piece of white bread with barbecue sauce and pile on some snouts. Top with an additional piece of bread.

7. Serve as a sandwich, but eat the snouts piece by piece with bits of the bread. Serve with additional sauce.

Makes 10 sandwiches.

TECHNIQUE: Direct and indirect heat	**RUB:** No
SMOKE: Charcoal or wood	**MOP:** No
TEMPERATURE: 225° to 275°F	**SAUCE:** Yes
TIME: 2 to 2½ hours	

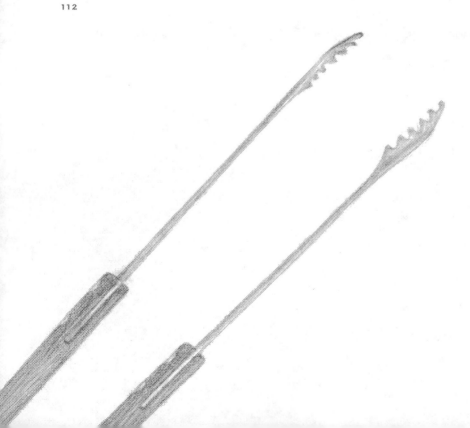

Barbecued Chicken
Halves or Quarters

Barbecuing chicken is easier if you use quarters or halves instead of whole chickens, which take longer to cook, or single serving pieces, which dry out easily. Don't even think about taking off the skin before cooking chicken. The fat under the skin is absolutely necessary for flavor and juicy tenderness. Peel it off before eating if you must, but if you taste even a morsel of crispy barbecued chicken skin, you won't want to.

Season chicken pieces generously with dry rub, place over very low coals, and be prepared to stand by. Chicken burns easily when the fat drops on the fire. Using a water smoker eliminates this problem, but if you want crispy skin, finish cooking directly over hot coals.

12 chicken quarters, breast or leg or a
    combination

Dry Rub for Chicken (page 119)

Chicken Barbecue Sauce (page 124)

1. Use enough coals (wood or a combination of wood and charcoal) to spread in a single layer over the bottom of the grill. Pile the coals together and light them. When the coals glow bright red and turn gray with ash, spread them in an even layer.

2. Meanwhile, rinse and dry the chicken pieces. Sprinkle dry rub generously on all sides and allow the chicken to come to room temperature while the fire is burning down to medium-low or low.

3. When the fire is ready, place the chicken, skin side down, on the grate. Cover with the lid and cook about 10 to 15 minutes, or until the skin begins to brown. Turn the chicken and cook until the other side begins to brown, about 10 to 15 minutes. If the coals flame up, squirt with water to douse.

4. Continue cooking and turning until the chicken has cooked about 45 minutes to 1 hour. By then, juices from the breast quarters will probably run clear, although there will still be some pink in the leg quarters. Move the breast quarters to the edges of the fire to prevent overcooking and drying out. Move the leg quarters to the hotter part of the grill. Brush all the pieces lightly with sauce and grill 10 to 15 minutes longer, turning once or twice and basting lightly with sauce. Try to baste sparingly so the sauce does not drip on the coals and cause flare-ups.

5. Remove the breast quarters when the juices run clear when a piece is pierced in the thickest

part. The leg quarters may take 5 to 10 minutes longer; the juices should run clear when a thigh is pierced in the thickest part.

6. Heat the remaining barbecue sauce and serve with the chicken.

Serves 6 to 8.

TECHNIQUE: Direct heat	**TIME:** 1 to 1¼ hours
SMOKE: Hickory, maple, oak, pecan, or other sweet wood	**RUB:** Yes
	MOP: No
TEMPERATURE: 300° to 350°F	**SAUCE:** Yes

Whole Barbecued Chicken

Whole barbecued chickens are often a Sunday-only offering at barbecue shacks—a remnant of that old Sunday chicken thing, I guess. Barbecued chicken, the really good stuff, draws from the flavor profile of Southern barbecue styles, generally sweeter and hotter than the smoky style developed in the Texas Hill Country for brisket.

If you're going to smoke a whole chicken, you might as well smoke two or three. The leftovers are great for barbecued chicken pizza, smoked chicken salad, or sandwiches. Chicken tastes particularly good when smoked with hickory.

1 to 3 whole fryers (about 3 pounds each)	Basting Sauce for Chicken (page 121), optional
Dry Rub for Chicken (page 119)	Chicken Barbecue Sauce (page 124)

1. Prepare a fire by lighting wood or a combination of wood and charcoal in the firebox of a cooker or at the end of a barrel smoker opposite the end with the vent or chimney. Or light the coals in a water smoker. Or preheat a gas smoker/grill.

2. When the fire has burned down to glowing embers or the coals are covered with gray ash, place the chicken at the end of the smoker near the chimney. Or place a full pan of water over the coals or hot lava rocks, then position the grate and the chicken.

3. Allow about 1 hour of cooking time per pound. Tack on time (in 30-minute intervals) as needed, depending on how fast the chickens cook. Even the outside temperature can affect cooking time, which is longer on cold days. If desired, baste the chicken with basting sauce every half hour after the first 30 minutes of cooking.

4. Tend the fire by adding wood or charcoal (or hot coals from a separate fire) to keep it from going out and to keep the temperature at the cooking end from getting too low; between 225° and 300°F.

5. The chicken is done when the juices run clear when the thick part of a thigh or leg is pierced with a fork or when the temperature registers 180°F on an instant-read thermometer. Remove the chicken from the heat and allow to rest for 10 minutes. It may be served hot or at room temperature, with barbecue sauce.

Serves 6 to 8.

THE BASICS

TECHNIQUE: Indirect heat

SMOKE: Hickory, maple, oak, pecan, or other sweet wood

TEMPERATURE: 225° to 300°F

TIME: 3 to 4 hours; up to 6 hours

RUB: Yes

MOP: Optional

SAUCE: Yes

Carolina-Style Mustard Barbecued Chicken

The flavors of Carolina take exceptionally well to chicken. This version, seasoned with a mustard baste, does not use the typical sweetish red sauce of other areas.

4 to 6 chicken quarters, leg or breast or a combination	Carolina Chicken Mop Sauce (page 120)
¼ cup vegetable oil	Salt and black pepper to taste

1. Use enough coals (wood or a combination of wood and charcoal) to spread in a single layer over the bottom of the grill. Pile the coals together and light them. When the coals glow bright red and begin to turn gray with ash, spread them in an even layer.

2. Meanwhile, rinse and dry the chicken pieces. Allow them to come to room temperature while the fire is burning down to medium-low or low.

3. When the fire is ready, lightly brush the chicken on all sides with oil. Add the remaining oil to the mop sauce. Place the chicken, skin side down, on the grate. Cover with the lid and cook about 10 to 15 minutes or until the skin begins to brown. Turn the chicken, cover with the lid, and cook until the other side browns.

4. Turn the chicken once more and baste with the sauce. Grill about 10 minutes, turn, and baste again. Continue cooking, turning and basting, until the chicken has cooked 1 hour to 1 hour 15 minutes and tests done. The juices should run clear when the chicken is pierced with a fork. If the breast quarters are done sooner than the leg quarters, move them to the edges of the fire to prevent overcooking and drying out. Move the leg quarters to the hotter part of the grill.

5. Remove the chicken to a platter and keep warm. Return the remaining mop sauce to low heat and bring to a boil. Add any juices that have accumulated from the cooked chicken. Taste and adjust the seasoning with salt and pepper. Pour the sauce over the chicken and serve.

Serves 4 to 6.

FAIL-SAFE TECHNIQUE: *If the chicken seems to be cooking too fast and burning (or you start to think it will never get done), preheat the oven to 350°F. Remove the chicken pieces to a shallow roasting pan, leaving plenty of space between them, and roast in the oven about 30 minutes. Test for doneness as above.*

TECHNIQUE: Direct heat	**RUB:** No
SMOKE: Hickory or oak	**MOP:** Yes
TEMPERATURE: 300° to 325°F	**SAUCE:** Optional
TIME: 1 to 1½ hours	

Lemon Barbecued Whole Fish

While fish is one of the least frequently barbecued foods, its delicate taste can be enhanced by a subtle sauce. A whole firm-fleshed fish will dry out the least and fulfill its flavor promise. It's also easier to handle.

Placing the fish on a flat pan before placing inside the cooker also makes the task easier. A dollop of Barbecue Mayonnaise tastes wonderful with the smoky fish.

This fish isn't true barbecue, since it is roasted over coals at a temperature too high for barbecuing.

2 to 3 lemons, sliced very thin, including rind	Juice of 1 to 2 lemons
1 3- to 5-pound salmon or red snapper or other firm-fleshed white fish	½ cup (1 stick) butter, melted
2 teaspoons coarse sea salt or to taste	1 tablespoon olive oil
2 teaspoons coarsely ground pepper or to taste	2 teaspoons paprika or to taste
	Barbecue Mayonnaise (page 125), optional

1. Prepare a fire using wood or a combination of wood and charcoal. The fire should be low, 300° to 325°F.

2. Meanwhile, line the bottom of a large, flat metal baking pan or fish grilling basket with a single layer of lemon slices. Rinse and dry the fish, inside and out. Season the inside of the fish with part of the salt and pepper and sprinkle with some lemon juice.

3. Cut 3 or 4 gashes on each side of the fish, cutting all the way to the bone. Combine the melted butter with the olive oil, 1 teaspoon each salt and pepper (or to taste), 1 to 2 tablespoons lemon juice, and the paprika. Brush the fish on all sides with the butter mixture, making sure plenty runs into the gashes. Place the fish directly on the lemon slices and pour the remaining butter mixture on top. Place a lemon slice over the fish's eye, if desired.

4. Cook the fish over direct heat, about 20 minutes per pound or until its flesh is white. Check one of the gashes in the thickest part of the fish. The meat should be white down to the biggest bone.

5. When the fish is done, carefully remove it from the pan and place on a warm serving platter. Loosely drape with foil to keep warm.

6. Remove the lemon slices from the pan juices. Strain the juices over the fish. To serve warm, use a spoon to scoop the flesh from one side of the fish; turn and scoop from the remaining side.

7. Serve warm with a dollop of Barbecue Mayonnaise, if desired.

Serves 4 to 6.

THE BASICS

TECHNIQUE: Direct heat	**RUB:** No
SMOKE: Charcoal or favorite wood	**MOP:** No
TEMPERATURE: 300° to 325°F	**SAUCE:** Optional
TIME: 1 to 1³/₄ hours	

Owensboro-Style Barbecue Rub

Allspice gives this a decidedly different flavor profile from other rubs. It really complements lamb.

¼ cup coarsely ground black pepper	1 tablespoon granulated garlic or garlic powder
2 tablespoons brown sugar	
1 tablespoon salt	¼ teaspoon ground allspice

Combine all the ingredients and store in an airtight container. Coat the meat on all sides before cooking.

Makes about ½ cup.

Dry Rub for Chicken

This seasoning blend is just the right mix of sweet and hot for chicken.

¼ cup sugar	1 tablespoon lemon pepper
1 tablespoon salt	1 tablespoon garlic powder
1 tablespoon finely ground black pepper	¼ teaspoon cayenne pepper
1 tablespoon paprika	

Combine all the ingredients in a jar with a tight-fitting lid. Shake to combine.

Makes about ½ cup.

Owensboro-Style Barbecue Mop

½ cup white vinegar	1 tablespoon brown sugar
½ cup water	2 teaspoons salt or to taste
½ cup beer or beef stock	2 teaspoons garlic powder
2 tablespoons Worcestershire sauce	½ teaspoon cayenne pepper or to taste
1 tablespoon coarsely ground black pepper	

Combine all the ingredients in a small saucepan over low heat. Cook and stir just until the mixture boils. Remove from the heat and cool.

Makes about 1½ cups.

Carolina Chicken Mop Sauce

Similar to a pork basting broth, this is piquant and highly acidic—great with chicken.

1½ cups chicken broth	2 to 3 sprigs fresh parsley
½ teaspoon red pepper flakes	1 bay leaf
1 teaspoon black peppercorns	¼ cup yellow mustard

In a small saucepan, combine the chicken broth, red pepper flakes, black peppercorns, parsley, and bay leaf and cook over very low heat for about 30 minutes. Remove the parsley and bay leaf. Stir in the mustard and heat through. Cool and refrigerate to store, up to 2 weeks.

Makes 1½ cups.

Basting Sauce
for Chicken

P unch up the heat factor on barbecued chicken with this basting sauce.

¼ cup lemon juice	2 teaspoons salt
½ cup vegetable oil, preferably corn oil	1 tablespoon red pepper sauce or to taste
½ cup cider vinegar	1 small bay leaf, crumbled
¾ cup beer	

Combine all the ingredients in a small saucepan over medium heat. Bring to a boil, lower the heat, and simmer for 30 minutes before using.

Makes 2 cups.

WILD

CARDS

121

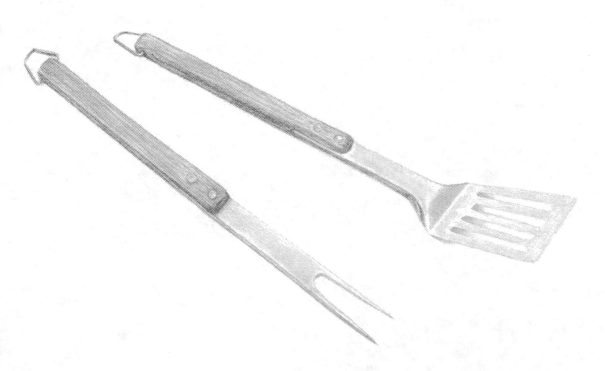

Owensboro-Style
Black Barbecue Dip

This pungent sauce is dark as a starless night. Its sweet, salty, sour contrast is the perfect foil for pungent lamb.

1 cup Worcestershire sauce

1 cup white vinegar

1/4 cup packed dark brown sugar

2 teaspoons salt or to taste

2 tablespoons lemon juice

1 teaspoon garlic powder or 1 clove garlic, finely chopped

1 teaspoon onion powder

1/2 teaspoon ground allspice

Combine all the ingredients in a small saucepan over low heat. When the liquid boils, reduce the heat and simmer for 10 minutes or until slightly thickened. Serve warm or at room temperature.

Makes about 2 cups.

 The simple fact is that all regional barbecue is good.
One region is just different from another.

——PAUL KIRK, *PAUL KIRK'S CHAMPIONSHIP BARBECUE SAUCES*

St. Louis
Barbecue Sauce

Use this thick sauce to coat the slices of bread served with snouts. The tangy elements of vinegar and mustard help cut the grease, while the sweet and spicy flavor notes enhance the crispy exterior of the rendered pork skin and fat. The sauce also goes well with pulled pork shoulder, chicken, or wet ribs.

1 32-ounce bottle ketchup	2 teaspoons black pepper
1 cup packed brown sugar	2 tablespoons Worcestershire sauce
¼ cup yellow mustard	1 tablespoon garlic salt
½ cup cider vinegar	
2 teaspoons Louisiana hot sauce or other red pepper sauce	

1. Combine all the ingredients in a small nonreactive saucepan over medium heat. Blend well. Bring the mixture to a boil, reduce the heat, and simmer for 20 to 30 minutes or until the sauce is shiny.

2. Serve warm. Store tightly covered in the refrigerator up to 3 weeks.

Makes about 3½ cups.

Chicken Barbecue Sauce

deal for serving with barbecued chicken, this table sauce also goes well with pork.

2 cups ketchup	2 teaspoons yellow mustard
2 8-ounce cans tomato sauce	2 tablespoons butter
½ cup packed brown sugar	1 teaspoon salt or to taste
1 tablespoon Worcestershire sauce	½ teaspoon black pepper or to taste
½ to 1 teaspoon hot sauce or to taste	1 to 2 tablespoons lemon juice or to taste

Combine all the ingredients in a medium saucepan. Stir and cook over low heat until well blended and bubbly. Set aside. Reheat at the edge of the grill during the last 30 to 60 minutes of barbecuing time for a smoky flavor. Be careful not to let the sauce burn. Remove it immediately if it starts to stick. Serve warm or at room temperature.

Makes about 4 cups.

Barbecue Mayonnaise

This is particularly good with barbecued whole fish. Try it also as a spread for sandwiches made with leftover beef brisket or pork.

½ cup mayonnaise	1 teaspoon grated onion
¼ cup bottled or homemade barbecue sauce	Salt and black pepper to taste
1 teaspoon finely grated lemon peel	1 tablespoon capers, drained, optional

In a small bowl, combine the mayonnaise, barbecue sauce, lemon peel, onion, salt, and pepper. Use a small whisk or fork to blend the ingredients. Fold in the capers, if desired.

Makes about ³/₄ cup.

Santa Maria Salsa

This salsa is so-o-o-o California, with celery, green onions, and mild Anaheim chilies. As a garnish to beautiful rosy slices of smoked tri-tip, it can't be beat. It also freshens and enhances pinquito beans.

3 medium tomatoes, chopped

½ cup finely chopped celery

½ cup finely chopped green onions, both white and green parts

½ cup finely chopped fresh California (Anaheim) green chilies

2 tablespoons chopped fresh cilantro

1 tablespoon white vinegar

Dash of Worcestershire sauce

½ teaspoon garlic salt

½ teaspoon dried oregano, crushed

A few drops red pepper sauce or to taste

In a nonreactive bowl, combine all the ingredients. Cover and let stand for 1 hour so the flavors blend.

Makes 3½ cups.

hot bites and sides

Barbecue is slow going, which means that the cook and everybody else will develop quite an appetite just inhaling the tantalizing aromas from the cooker. Chances are, no matter how you planned the timing, the barbecue usually has "another hour" to go. Since you've probably got a second grill going to fuel the fire under the barbecue, make use of those hot coals to fire up some hot bites to make the wait easier. Be sure to offer a cold beverage to cool things off. Another way to kill waiting time is to get busy in the kitchen making side dishes and desserts.

The go-withs for barbecue are infinite. Traditional dishes like beans, coleslaw, and potato salad span the regions. Some dishes may be remarkably similar from Carolina to Texas. For example, virtually all regions love mayonnaise potato salad with varying degrees of mustard blended in. But all along the way there are permutations unique to specific regions, even to geographic areas within the regions.

When there's only one vegetable side for barbecue, it is slaw. Like the main event, it comes in many variations. The cabbage may be grated, chopped, or shredded. The dressing may be creamy or vinegary. For the most strictly prescribed styles, look to the Carolinas, where a mayonnaise-based dressing gets the nod in the east and red slaw holds sway in the Piedmont. To be authentic, Carolina-style slaw must be finely grated using a hand grater or food processor.

Beans are another common barbecue go-with. In a blind tasting, the flavor of the beans could provide good clues about the region they come from, since the seasonings usually reflect those of the barbecue.

Along the Atlantic seaboard, beans are more likely to be baked and have a sweeter flavor profile, especially in the Deep South. The farther west along the barbecue trail, the more savory and spicy beans become. In Texas they'll probably be boiled in a big pot instead of baked. Navy beans are usually the beans of choice for baking, slathered with ketchup, mustard, and brown sugar. From the stovetop, pinto beans seasoned with onions and garlic waft their equally enticing aroma.

While salad is what many barbecue lovers envision when they think of potatoes, there are other ways to cook the noble spud as well. Just as there are schools of barbecue, there are schools of potato salad—the mustard and the mayo camps—guided more by personal preference than by regional tradition.

Plain boiled potatoes are often the choice with Carolina-style barbecue. Just

peel, boil, and eat, salting generously along the way. But there's a jazzed-up local variation as well: In parts of North Carolina, barbecued potatoes—potatoes flavored with a Piedmont-style barbecue sauce in the cooking liquid—are traditional.

And of course, mashed potatoes are a perfect go-with anytime meat is on the menu. While not a long-standing regional treatment, "smashed" potatoes with cheese may become one of your favorites. They're particularly appealing with beef brisket.

In the South, specifically the Carolinas, cornbread or hushpuppies are almost as necessary as slaw on a plate or tray of barbecue. Cornbread is oven-baked cornmeal batter with varying degrees of sweetness. Hushpuppies are rounds or rods of stiffer cornmeal batter that are deep-fried until golden and crisp. Cornbread also goes great with bean dishes, burgoo, and Brunswick stew, the dish that Carolinians love with barbecue.

Fried onion rings sit like golden crowns on many styles of barbecue. No chapter on sides would be complete without them.

Beef or
Chicken Bites

These grilled morsels can be prepared as small appetizers: single cubes of beef or chicken wrapped with bacon and secured with toothpicks. For kebabs, thread two or three pieces of meat on a skewer, intertwined with bacon and pieces of jalapeño pepper.

You could serve these as a main course, but don't kid yourself. This *isn't* barbecue.

1½ to 2 pounds boneless beef sirloin or boneless, skinless chicken breasts

½ cup vegetable oil

3 cloves garlic, crushed

⅓ cup pineapple or orange juice

2 teaspoons soy sauce or to taste

1 teaspoon red pepper flakes or to taste

4 to 6 fresh jalapeño peppers

6 to 8 strips of lean bacon, cut in half

12 to 16 toothpicks or skewers or more as needed

1. Rinse the beef or chicken and pat dry. Trim any fat from the meat and cut into 12 to 16 2-inch cubes. Combine the oil, garlic, juice, soy sauce, and red pepper flakes in a nonreactive bowl or a plastic bag. Add the beef or chicken. Stir (or shake the bag) to coat evenly and marinate for at least 1 hour or overnight.

2. Carefully trim off the stem end of the peppers and cut them in half lengthwise. Using the tip of a paring knife, remove the seeds and membranes. Cut the peppers into thin strips. (Use caution when handling fresh chile peppers; wear plastic gloves and be careful not to touch your eyes or mouth after handling.)

3. Remove the beef or chicken from the marinade and drain. Place 2 or 3 strips of pepper on a piece of bacon. Lay a marinated cube on the bacon and tightly wrap the bacon around the meat. Secure with toothpicks or skewers. Repeat for the remaining ingredients.

4. Prepare a fire using enough coals to form a 2-inch layer in the bottom of a grill. Arrange the coals in a pyramid shape and light. When the coals burn down and begin to turn gray, spread into an even layer. Or preheat a grill to medium-hot.

5. Grill the bacon-wrapped bites over medium-hot coals for 15 to 20 minutes, turning so all

sides are cooked evenly, until the beef is medium or the chicken juices run clear. The bacon should be crisp at the edges.

6. Serve warm or at room temperature.

Makes 12 to 16 pieces; serves 6 to 8 as an appetizer or 3 to 4 as an entrée.

Smoked or Grilled Oysters

A great use for the fire-maintenance grill is heating fresh oysters just enough to make them pop open. Or if it's time to check the meat (and you'll be opening the cooker anyway), throw some oysters on the cooking grate. Their shells will open slightly after just a few minutes over hot coals or in the cooker. Wear heavy gloves to remove the oysters from the grill. Take off the top shell and serve on the half-shell.

24 to 32 oysters (or more if you're serving oyster lovers!)	Bottled red pepper sauce or seafood cocktail sauce
Fresh lemon slices	Caramelized Onions (page 146), optional

1. Rinse the oysters to clean their shells. Discard any that have open shells.

2. Wearing heavy gloves, place the oysters in the cooker or over hot coals. Check after 3 to 5 minutes. When the shells open, remove the oysters from the cooker. Pry off the top shell, being careful to retain the juices, along with the oyster, in the bottom shell.

3. Serve with fresh lemon slices and red pepper sauce or seafood cocktail sauce. These oysters are also delicious with a dollop of caramelized onions.

Serves 6 to 8.

Eastern North Carolina Coleslaw

Some versions of this style of slaw use white or very pale green cabbage so finely ground it looks like grits or couscous.

Serve as a side to pulled, chopped barbecued pork or on top of the meat in a Carolina-style pulled pork sandwich.

1/2 head green cabbage (about 3/4 pound), to make 4 to 5 cups shredded	1 tablespoon yellow mustard
2 tablespoons cider vinegar	1 teaspoon celery seeds, optional
1/3 cup sugar	1/2 teaspoon salt or to taste
3/4 cup mayonnaise	1/8 teaspoon black pepper or to taste

1. Remove the outer leaves from the cabbage and cut out the core. Refrigerate the cabbage until ready to grate.

2. In a small bowl, stir together the vinegar and sugar. Stir until the sugar is dissolved. Whisk in the mayonnaise, mustard, celery seeds, salt, and pepper.

3. Finely grate or shred the cabbage using a hand grater, grinder, or food processor. The cabbage may be as fine as grits or couscous or as coarse as whole oats. Place in a large bowl.

4. Stir in the dressing. Taste and adjust the seasonings. Mix thoroughly, cover, and refrigerate at least 1 hour before serving. Drain off any excess dressing before serving so that the dressing will not run on a plate or make a sandwich soggy.

Serves 8 to 10.

Red Slaw
Piedmont Style

This is the orange-red coleslaw found in the western part of North Carolina. As a general rule, the cabbage is grated about the size of whole oats or BBs.

½ head green cabbage (about ¾ pound), to make 4 to 5 cups shredded	½ teaspoon salt or to taste
½ cup cider vinegar	1 teaspoon black pepper or to taste
¼ cup sugar	1 to 2 teaspoons red pepper sauce or to taste
⅓ cup ketchup	

1. Remove the outer leaves from the cabbage and cut out the core. Refrigerate the cabbage until ready to grate.

2. In a small bowl, stir together the vinegar, sugar, ketchup, salt, black pepper, and red pepper sauce. Stir until the sugar is dissolved.

3. Finely grate or shred the cabbage using a hand grater, grinder, or food processor. The cabbage should be about the size of whole oats. Place in a large bowl.

4. Stir in the dressing. Taste and adjust the seasonings. Mix well, cover, and refrigerate at least 1 hour. Don't worry if the cabbage appears dry at first. As it wilts and natural juices accumulate, there will be plenty of dressing to moisten the cabbage. Drain off any excess dressing or juices before serving so that the liquid doesn't run on a plate or make a sandwich soggy.

Serves 8 to 10.

SHORTCUT: *In place of the dressing, pour red Western North Carolina (Piedmont)–Style Barbecue Sauce (page 42) over shredded cabbage and refrigerate several hours or overnight.*

Creamy Coleslaw

This creamy slaw works well as a side with Texas, Memphis, or Kansas City barbecue. The shredded cabbage isn't as finely grated as in the Carolinas. Heck, rough chop it if you want.

½ head green cabbage (about ¾ pound), to make 4 to 5 cups shredded	1 tablespoon cider vinegar
½ cup mayonnaise	1 teaspoon salt or to taste
2 tablespoons sugar	1 teaspoon black pepper or to taste

1. Remove the outer leaves from the cabbage and cut out the core. Refrigerate the cabbage until ready to shred.

2. In a small bowl, stir together the mayonnaise, sugar, vinegar, salt, and pepper. Stir until the sugar is dissolved.

3. Shred or chop the cabbage. Place in a large bowl. Pour the dressing over the cabbage and mix well. Refrigerate 1 hour.

Serves 8 to 10.

Sweet-Sour Coleslaw

Some people like a vinaigrette-style dressing such as this one. It's particularly nice with barbecued chicken.

½ head green cabbage (about ¾ pound), to make 4 to 5 cups shredded	½ cup vegetable oil
½ cup cider vinegar	1 teaspoon salt
⅓ cup sugar	¾ teaspoon celery seeds, optional

1. Remove the outer leaves from the cabbage and cut out the core. Refrigerate the cabbage until ready to shred or chop.

2. In a small bowl, stir together the vinegar and sugar until the sugar is dissolved. Whisk in the vegetable oil and salt. Add the celery seeds, if desired.

3. Chop or shred the cabbage. Place in a large bowl. Pour the dressing over the cabbage and mix well. Refrigerate 1 to 3 hours.

Serves 8 to 10.

Leafy Greens, Pears, and Pecans with Sherry Vinaigrette

This isn't a traditional salad for barbecue, but it is a nice change. It also goes well with grilled Beef or Chicken Bites (page 129) or a juicy steak.

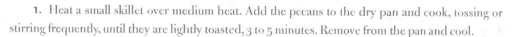

½ cup pecan pieces	⅓ cup crumbled blue or Roquefort cheese
1 12-ounce package mixed leafy greens	
1 Bartlett or other ripe pear	Sherry Vinaigrette (page 136)

1. Heat a small skillet over medium heat. Add the pecans to the dry pan and cook, tossing or stirring frequently, until they are lightly toasted, 3 to 5 minutes. Remove from the pan and cool.

2. Place the greens in a salad bowl. Core the pear but do not peel. Cut into ½-inch pieces. Toss the pear and crumbled cheese with the greens. Just before serving, pour the dressing over the salad and toss to coat everything evenly.

3. Sprinkle the toasted pecans over the top of the salad.

Serves 4 (doubles easily).

VARIATION: *Substitute 1 cup chopped mandarin oranges or fresh tangerines for the pear and ½ cup toasted almonds for the pecans. Omit cheese.*

Sherry Vinaigrette

½ cup extra virgin olive oil

2 tablespoons sherry vinegar

1 tablespoon finely chopped shallots

½ teaspoon salt

¼ teaspoon black pepper

In a small bowl or a jar with a tight-fitting lid, combine all the ingredients. Stir or shake vigorously to combine.

Makes scant ¾ cup, or 4 servings.

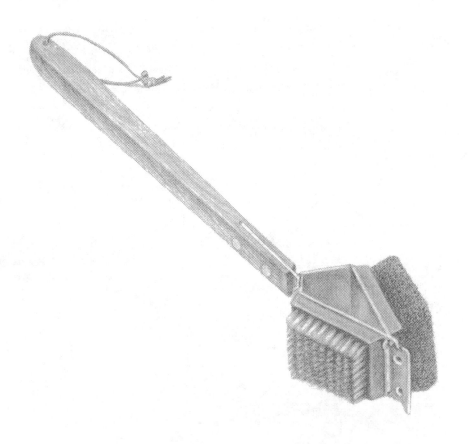

Barbecue
Baked Beans

Relatively sweet, this style of baked beans is popular in the Midwest.

⅓ cup firmly packed brown sugar	2 teaspoons yellow mustard
½ cup homemade or bottled barbecue sauce	3 16-ounce cans pork and beans, undrained
¼ cup ketchup	½ cup chopped onion
½ teaspoon salt	3 slices bacon, cooked, drained, and crumbled, or ½ cup trimmings from smoked beef brisket or pork shoulder
1 teaspoon black pepper	
2 tablespoons molasses	

1. Preheat the oven to 350°F. Lightly grease a 2½-quart baking dish.

2. In a large bowl, combine the brown sugar, barbecue sauce, ketchup, salt, black pepper, molasses, and mustard. Stir until the sugar is dissolved. Add the pork and beans, onion, and bacon or trimmings, mixing well.

3. Pour the beans into the prepared dish. Bake for 1 hour, uncovered, stirring once.

Serves 10.

Cowboy Pinto Beans

A big pot of pinto beans can usually be found simmering on the stove in a Texas barbecue restaurant or a ranch kitchen. They're a traditional side with beef brisket.

1 pound dried pinto beans	1 fresh jalapeño pepper, optional
2 cups chopped onions	1 teaspoon salt or to taste
2 cloves garlic, crushed	3 tablespoons chopped fresh cilantro, optional
½ cup uncooked bacon or barbecue trimmings cut into 1-inch pieces	

1. Rinse the beans in a colander. Place in a large saucepan or stockpot with enough water to cover. Bring to a boil over high heat and cook for 1 minute; turn off the heat, cover, and let the beans soak for 1 hour. Or soak the beans (uncooked) overnight.

2. When the beans have finished soaking, pour off the soaking liquid. Remove the beans from the pot, rinse the pot, and return the beans. Add the onions, garlic, bacon or trimmings, and enough water to cover by 1 inch. Add the jalapeño if you want the heat.

3. Bring the water to a boil over high heat. Lower the heat, cover, and simmer 2 to 3 hours or until the beans are tender. When beans are tender, add the salt. Just before serving, add the cilantro, if desired.

Serves 10.

SHORTCUT: *In a medium saucepan, combine 4 15-ounce cans of pinto beans, undrained, with the onions, garlic, bacon or trimmings, and jalapeño (if desired). Bring the liquid to a boil, lower the heat, and simmer, covered, for 1 hour, stirring occasionally.*

Santa Maria–Style Pinquito Beans

These are the signature beans of the Santa Maria style of barbecue. Similar in color to pinto beans, but about half the size, pinquito beans are unique to the Santa Maria Valley in California. They are available by mail order from Righetti Specialties, Inc., 7476 Graciosa Rd., Santa Maria, CA 94355; phone: 805-937-2402. Or substitute pinto beans.

1 pound dried pinquito beans	¼ cup chili sauce
1 strip bacon, chopped	1 tablespoon sugar
½ cup chopped ham	1 teaspoon dry mustard
1 clove garlic, finely chopped	1 teaspoon salt
¾ cup tomato puree	

1. Rinse the beans and remove any small stones or shriveled beans. Place in a large bowl or saucepan, add enough water to cover, and soak overnight. After soaking, drain the beans, place in a large saucepan, and add enough fresh water to cover.

2. Bring the water to a boil over high heat. Lower the heat, cover, and simmer 2 hours or until tender.

3. Meanwhile, cook the bacon and ham in a small skillet over medium heat until browned. Add the garlic and cook 1 to 2 minutes, stirring frequently. Add the tomato puree, chili sauce, sugar, mustard, and salt. Stir and remove from the heat.

4. Drain most of the liquid from the beans and stir the sauce into them. Heat through and keep warm until ready to serve.

Serves 8 to 10.

Red Beans and Rice

Red beans and rice go with barbecue when Cajuns are doing the cooking or in any region where rice is a staple. Use Louisiana red beans, not kidney beans. If they are not available in your area, you can order them from www.BulkFoods.com.

8 ounces dried small red beans	¼ pound salt pork or 4 slices bacon
2 bay leaves	1 cup chopped onion
1 teaspoon dried thyme	1 clove garlic, finely chopped
1 cup uncooked white rice	1 teaspoon salt or to taste

1. Rinse the beans and remove any small stones or shriveled beans. Place the rinsed beans in a large saucepan or stewpot and add enough water to cover. Bring the water to a boil over high heat. Boil for 5 minutes, then drain the beans.

2. Remove the beans from the pot, rinse the pot, and return the beans. Add enough water to cover by 1 inch. Stir in the bay leaves and thyme. Bring the water to a boil, lower the heat, cover, and cook until the beans are tender, about 2 hours. Check occasionally to make sure the water does not cook away; add more as needed. The cooking liquid should be allowed to reduce enough to thicken slightly. When the beans are tender, lower the heat to a simmer and remove the lid so the liquid continues to thicken.

3. Meanwhile, place the rice in a microwave-safe bowl with 2 cups water. Cover and cook on high for 5 minutes. Continue cooking on medium (50 percent) power for 15 minutes or until the rice is tender and most of the water is evaporated. Set aside and keep warm.

4. Cut the salt pork or bacon into small (½-inch) pieces. In a skillet over high heat, cook the salt pork or bacon until the fat begins to melt. Add the onion and garlic. Lower the heat and cook until the onion is soft, about 5 minutes.

5. Stir the cooked salt pork or bacon and onion into the beans. Allow to simmer 10 to 20 minutes. Taste and add salt if needed. Serve over the rice, or stir the rice into the beans.

Serves 4 to 6.

Potato Salad with Mayonnaise and Hard-Cooked Eggs

For mayonnaise lovers, this is the real deal: lots of mayo with some sour cream for velvety texture and hard-cooked eggs for color. Green onions give it oomph. It's great with dry ribs or brisket.

2 pounds russet potatoes (4 to 5), unpeeled	¼ cup chopped green onions, both white and green parts
2 teaspoons salt or to taste	1 teaspoon black pepper or to taste
½ cup mayonnaise	3 hard-cooked eggs
⅓ cup sour cream	¼ cup finely chopped parsley, for garnish

1. Place the potatoes in a large saucepan with enough cold water to cover. Add the salt and bring the water to a boil over high heat. Cover the pan, lower the heat, and cook until the potatoes are easily pierced with a fork all the way to the middle, 20 to 30 minutes, depending on the size of the potatoes. Drain the potatoes and cool enough to handle easily.

2. Peel and cut the potatoes into bite-size (about 1-inch) cubes. Place in a large bowl.

3. Stir together the mayonnaise, sour cream, green onions, and black pepper. Fold the dressing into the potatoes and toss gently to coat evenly. Taste and adjust the seasonings.

4. Separate the yolks and whites of 2 eggs and coarsely chop. Gently fold into the salad.

5. Cut the remaining egg into thin rounds or wedges and use to decorate the top edge of the potato salad. Sprinkle the center with chopped parsley. Cover tightly and chill at least 1 hour.

Serves 8 to 10.

Mustard
Potato Salad

A touch of mustard, and dill pickle juice, make this a more piquant potato salad. It is the perfect foil for sweet barbecue like pork or chicken.

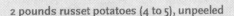

2 pounds russet potatoes (4 to 5), unpeeled	1/2 cup mayonnaise
2 teaspoons salt or to taste	2 tablespoons prepared mustard
1/2 cup chopped green onions, both white and green parts	1 tablespoon juice from dill pickles
1/2 cup chopped celery	1 teaspoon black pepper
2 tablespoons chopped pimiento	Paprika, for garnish
1/3 cup chopped dill pickle	

1. Place the potatoes in a large saucepan with enough cold water to cover. Add the salt and bring the water to a boil over high heat. Cover the pan, lower the heat, and cook until the potatoes are easily pierced with a fork all the way to the middle, 20 to 30 minutes, depending on the size of the potatoes. Drain the potatoes and cool enough to handle easily.

2. Peel and cut the potatoes into bite-size (about 1-inch) cubes. Place in a large bowl. Toss the potatoes with the green onions, celery, pimiento, and dill pickle.

3. Stir together the mayonnaise, mustard, pickle juice, and pepper. Fold the dressing into the potato mixture and toss gently to coat all the ingredients. Taste and adjust the seasonings.

4. Cover tightly and chill at least 1 hour. Sprinkle the top with paprika just before serving.

Serves 8 to 10.

Carolina Barbecue Potatoes

The potatoes soak up the flavorings in the cooking liquid; they are a light tomato-red color.

2 pounds russet potatoes (4 to 5), peeled	1 tablespoon red pepper sauce or to taste
1 large yellow onion	1 tablespoon sugar
1 tablespoon bacon drippings	1 teaspoon salt or to taste
½ cup ketchup	½ teaspoon black pepper or to taste

1. Cut the potatoes and onion into large chunks, about 2 inches. Place the chunks in a large pot and add enough water to cover. Add the bacon drippings, ketchup, red pepper sauce, sugar, salt, and black pepper, stirring to blend.

2. Over high heat, bring the water to a boil. Lower the heat and simmer until the potatoes are very soft, 20 to 30 minutes. Remove from the heat and let stand about 30 minutes or until the potatoes absorb most of the liquid. Heat again until bubbly; serve immediately.

Serves 6 to 8.

Smashed Potatoes with Cheese

Few things are better with meat, especially brisket, than potatoes with cheese. This recipe fits the bill perfectly.

2 pounds waxy white or yellow (not russet) potatoes (6 to 8), unpeeled	½ cup milk or as needed
3 teaspoons salt or to taste	1 cup grated cheddar cheese
2 tablespoons butter	½ cup chopped green onions, both white and green parts
¼ cup sour cream	1 teaspoon black pepper or to taste
3 ounces cream cheese	

1. Place the potatoes in a large saucepan with enough cold water to cover. Add 2 teaspoons of the salt and bring the water to a boil over high heat. Cover the pan, lower the heat, and cook until the potatoes are easily pierced with a fork, 15 to 20 minutes, depending on the size of the potatoes.

2. Meanwhile, preheat the oven to 325°F.

3. Drain the potatoes and return to the saucepan. Over low heat, shake the pan vigorously for 1 to 2 minutes to evaporate the remaining cooking water.

4. Off the heat, mash the potatoes with their skins. Do not mash until smooth; the potatoes should be chunky. Stir in the butter, sour cream, cream cheese, and just enough milk to give the potatoes a creamy consistency. Fold in ¾ cup of the grated cheese, the green onions, and 1 teaspoon each salt and pepper. Taste and adjust the seasonings.

5. Turn the potatoes into a 9 x 13-inch baking dish. Sprinkle the remaining cheese over the top. Place in the oven just long enough to melt the cheese. The casserole may be refrigerated at this point. To reheat, bake at 325°F for 20 to 30 minutes or until heated through.

Serves 6 to 8.

Smoked Potatoes
with Caramelized Onions

Cook these potatoes in the cooker alongside the beef or chicken with which you'll serve them. Consider substituting sweet potatoes and pairing this dish with pork.

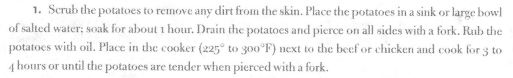

6 to 8 large baking potatoes or sweet potatoes, all about the same size and shape	Caramelized Onions (page 146)
	½ cup crumbled crisp-fried bacon, optional
Vegetable or olive oil	

1. Scrub the potatoes to remove any dirt from the skin. Place the potatoes in a sink or large bowl of salted water; soak for about 1 hour. Drain the potatoes and pierce on all sides with a fork. Rub the potatoes with oil. Place in the cooker (225° to 300°F) next to the beef or chicken and cook for 3 to 4 hours or until the potatoes are tender when pierced with a fork.

2. When the potatoes are tender, open and fluff them as you would baked potatoes. Serve with a spoonful of caramelized onions and a sprinkling of bacon, if desired.

Serves 6 to 8.

SHORTCUT: *Preheat the oven to 425°F. Scrub, soak, pierce, and oil the potatoes as directed above. Place directly on a rack in the hot oven and bake for 1 hour or until the potatoes yield slightly when pressed with an oven-mitted hand. Keep warm until serving time.*

Caramelized Onions

A spoonful of these onions on lightly roasted fresh oysters is a real treat. They also go well on any barbecued meat or a grilled steak.

1 large white or yellow onion, peeled and sliced very thin	1 tablespoon balsamic or sherry vinegar
	1 teaspoon maple syrup, optional
1 small red onion, peeled and sliced very thin	$^1/_2$ teaspoon salt or to taste
	$^1/_2$ teaspoon black pepper or to taste
1 tablespoon butter	
1 tablespoon olive oil	

1. Separate the thin onion slices into rings. Melt the butter in a skillet or saucepan over low heat; add the olive oil. Stir in the onions, coating evenly with the butter and oil. Cook and stir over low heat until the onions are soft. They should not brown. Stir in the vinegar and, if desired, the maple syrup.

2. Place a layer of wax paper directly on the onions and cover the skillet with a lid. Cook over low heat, stirring occasionally, until the onions are light brown and the cooking liquid is thickened and slightly syrupy, about 10 minutes. Season with the salt and pepper.

3. Serve warm or at room temperature.

Makes about 1$^1/_2$ to 2 cups.

Macaroni and Cheese
for Santa Maria Barbecue

This recipe is adapted from the "official" version attributed to the Santa Maria Valley traditionalists who serve it with that region's distinctive style of barbecue. This basic version also tastes great as a side dish for any kind of barbecue.

1½ cups elbow macaroni	⅛ teaspoon pepper
2 tablespoons butter	1½ cups shredded sharp cheddar cheese
2 tablespoons flour	2 cups hot milk
¾ teaspoon salt	

1. Preheat the oven to 350°F. Coat a 1½-quart casserole with cooking spray.

2. Heat a large pot of water. When the water boils, add the macaroni, stirring vigorously. Cook according to package directions, about 10 minutes. Drain the macaroni and set aside.

3. In a medium saucepan with a heavy bottom, melt the butter over low heat. Stir in the flour, salt, and pepper. Add 1 cup of the cheese to the hot milk and stir until melted. Slowly add the milk mixture to the butter and flour, stirring constantly. Cook and stir over very low heat until the cheese sauce is thickened and bubbly. Remove the sauce from the heat and combine it with the cooked macaroni in the prepared casserole. Sprinkle with the remaining ½ cup cheese. Bake for 35 to 40 minutes.

Serves 6 to 8.

SHORTCUT: *Cook the macaroni according to the package directions. Preheat the oven and prepare a 1½-quart casserole as directed above. Drain and return the macaroni to the hot pan. Cut a small log (10 ounces) of processed American cheese into large cubes. Stir into the hot macaroni, add ½ cup milk, and place over low heat. Stir and cook until the cheese melts. Stir in ½ cup shredded cheddar or American cheese. Turn the macaroni into the prepared casserole. Bake 20 to 30 minutes or until bubbly and browned at the edges.*

Hushpuppies

A touch of finely grated onion gives these cornmeal fritters some character.

2 cups white cornmeal	1 egg, lightly beaten
½ cup all-purpose flour	1 tablespoon finely grated onion, optional
1 tablespoon baking powder	2 cups buttermilk
1 teaspoon salt	Vegetable or corn oil

1. In a medium bowl, combine the cornmeal, flour, baking powder, and salt. Stir with a fork to blend. Add the egg, onion (if using), and buttermilk, stirring until thoroughly mixed. Allow the dough to rest for 5 minutes.

2. Meanwhile, pour oil into a large skillet to a depth of about 3 inches. Heat the oil to 350°F.

3. When the oil is hot, scoop a heaping tablespoon of dough into lightly oiled hands. Roll the dough between your palms into a cylinder about 2 inches long, or shape into balls about the size of golf balls. Carefully lower the hushpuppies into the hot oil. As they float, turn them to brown evenly. Drain on paper towels.

Makes about 2 dozen.

Carolina
Skillet Cornbread

Baked and cut into slabs, this cornbread is countrified by the addition of some drippings from pork barbecue and maybe some cracklings, luscious, crisp pieces of pork fat. With no leavening other than that in the self-rising cornmeal, this formula produces a flat, chewy style of cornbread.

2 tablespoons pork barbecue drippings,
    bacon drippings, or vegetable oil

1 1/2 cups self-rising cornmeal (preferably
    white cornmeal)

1/2 teaspoon salt

1 1/4 cups whole milk

2 tablespoons finely chopped cracklings
    or pork barbecue, optional

HOT BITES
AND SIDES
149

1. Preheat the oven to 500°F. Place a 9- or 10-inch black cast-iron skillet (or 9- or 10-inch round or square baking pan) in the oven while it heats.

2. When the oven is hot, remove the skillet and place the drippings in it. Swirl the drippings around the skillet to coat it evenly.

3. In a medium bowl, stir together the cornmeal, salt, and milk. Mix quickly, just to moisten the ingredients. Add the cracklings or meat, if using.

4. Pour the batter into the hot skillet and place in the oven. Lower the oven temperature to 450°F and bake the cornbread about 20 minutes or until golden brown.

5. To serve, cut into wedges or squares.

Serves 6 to 8.

Batter-Fried Onion Rings

Onion rings are to french fries as ribs are to barbecue—something special. Not just every barbecue restaurant makes 'em, and some that do don't do it very well. But there's nothing better than a fresh, steaming-hot, french-fried onion ring.

2 large sweet onions (4 to 6 inches in diameter)	1/2 teaspoon salt or to taste
1 cup buttermilk or as needed	1/4 teaspoon black pepper or to taste
2 cups dry pancake mix or as needed	Vegetable oil for deep-frying

1. Peel the onions and slice into thick rings about 3/4 inch wide. Separate the rings and place them in a shallow bowl or dish. Reserve the smallest rings for another use. Pour the buttermilk over the onion rings and soak for 30 minutes. If needed, add more buttermilk to generously coat the onions.

2. Place the pancake mix in a shallow bowl. Stir in the salt and pepper. Lift the onion rings from the buttermilk a few at a time, shaking off the excess liquid, and coat on all sides with the seasoned pancake mix. Place the battered rings in a single layer on wax paper. Do not allow their sides to touch.

3. When all the rings are coated, pour oil into a heavy saucepan or deep fryer and heat to 375°F. Drop a few rings at a time into the hot oil and cook until golden on all sides, turning once if necessary.

4. Drain on absorbent paper and keep warm while frying the remaining onion rings.

Serves 4 to 6.

sweet endings

pies, cakes, and other regional favorites

Desserts for barbecue should be as full-flavored and soulful as the main course.

Just about anything sweet is a good finish to a barbecue, but there are several homestyle desserts that are traditional. If there is such a thing as a universal barbecue dessert, it is banana pudding. Peach cobbler with vanilla ice cream is a close runner-up.

Still, there is something to be said for pie, which can be found in great variety in barbecue restaurants. The offerings usually include Southern staples like sweet potato, vinegar, chocolate, and chess pies. Barbecue restaurants and pies go together like pork and smoke.

Homespun and comforting, pies are a fine finale for barbecue. Since barbecue takes a while, making pie is a good time-killer during the long hours of waiting and watching while the barbecue cooks. Pie is also a no-brainer to serve once it's done, a definite plus in barbecue restaurants where a big service staff isn't part of the overhead.

Cake lovers may find satisfaction in a chocolate layer cake or a moist pound cake. What could be a more decadent finish to the decadence of barbecue than layers of chocolate cake and frosting? Not quite as spectacular but no less delicious, pound cake makes a good to-go dessert after a barbecue lunch, when the time constraints of getting back to work—or home for a nap—make lingering over the meal impractical.

Peach Cream Pie

Nothing is better in the summer than a fresh peach pie, especially one made from Texas or Georgia peaches. This recipe from Gail Hearn Plummer dates to the 1930s, perhaps farther back than that. "When times were tough in the Hearn house, my grandmother [Barbara Hearn of Freeport, Texas] still made peach cream pie; it's just that sometimes she made it without the peaches. No matter. They [her husband and eight children] loved it." Gail grew up on the version her mother, Georgia, made, which remains a tradition in Gail's Dallas home today.

½ recipe Homemade Pie Crust (page 157), unbaked, or a prepared crust

5 to 6 fresh peaches

⅔ to ¾ cup sugar

3 rounded tablespoons flour

3 tablespoons heavy cream

¼ cup (½ stick) butter, cut into small pieces about the size of a pea

½ teaspoon ground cinnamon

1. Preheat the oven to 300°F. Line a 10-inch pie pan with the pastry.

2. Peel the peaches, cut in half, and remove the pit. Crowd the peach halves, pit side up, in the bottom of the pie shell, with sides touching. Do not layer.

3. Combine the sugar and flour; sprinkle evenly over the peaches so that the mixture falls on the surface of the peaches and into crevices between the fruit. Drizzle the cream over the peaches as evenly as possible. Scatter the pieces of butter over the peaches and sprinkle with the cinnamon.

4. Bake for about 1½ hours. The pie should look slightly chewy around the edges.

Serves 8.

Sweet Potato Pie

No pie is more Southern than this smooth favorite, similar to pumpkin pie but with an extra jolt of natural sugar. Great with barbecue, it is also the perfect finish for a Thanksgiving meal or any other time when summer tree fruits are out of season.

½ recipe Homemade Pie Crust (page 157), unbaked, or a prepared crust	1 cup sugar
2 cups drained and mashed canned yams	1 teaspoon ground cinnamon
2 eggs, well beaten	1 teaspoon vanilla
¾ cup milk	¼ teaspoon salt
¼ cup (½ stick) butter, melted	

1. Preheat the oven to 350°F. Line a 9-inch pie pan with the pastry.

2. In a large bowl, combine the mashed sweet potatoes, eggs, milk, and butter, mixing well. Stir in the sugar, cinnamon, vanilla, and salt. Pour into the pie shell. Bake for 55 minutes to 1 hour or until the tip of a sharp knife inserted in the center comes out clean. Cool on a wire rack.

Serves 8.

Vinegar Pie

Sweet-and-sour is a marvelous combination to refresh the palate after a big plate of barbecue. Similar to a lemon chess pie, this vinegar pie satisfies the yen for a post-barbecue tang.

½ recipe Homemade Pie Crust (page 157) unbaked, or a prepared crust	3 eggs, well beaten
1½ cups sugar	2 tablespoons white vinegar
½ cup (1 stick) butter, melted	1 teaspoon vanilla

1. Preheat the oven to 325°F. Line a 9-inch pie pan with the pastry.

2. In a medium bowl, combine the sugar and melted butter. Blend on low speed with an electric mixer until the sugar is dissolved. Add the eggs, vinegar, and vanilla, beating on low speed until well blended, about 2 minutes. Pour the mixture into the pie shell.

3. Bake for 50 minutes or until the filling is golden brown and the tip of a sharp knife inserted in the center comes out clean. Serve warm or at room temperature.

Serves 8.

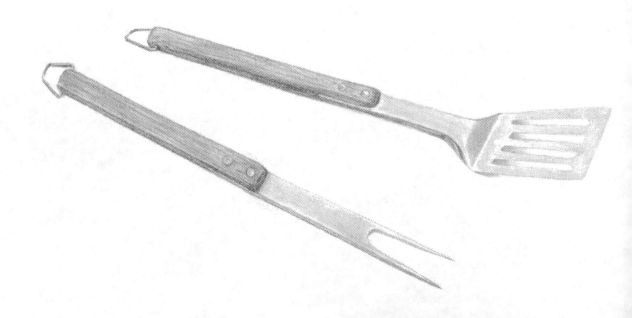

Lemon Chess Pie

Here's the real thing, lemon chess pie, a Southern classic with a filling similar to lemon curd. The sweet-and-sour balance truly refreshes and cools.

½ recipe Homemade Pie Crust (page 157), unbaked, or a prepared crust

2 cups sugar

1 tablespoon flour

1 tablespoon cornmeal

4 eggs, well beaten

¼ cup (½ stick) butter, melted

¼ cup milk

¼ cup lemon juice

2 teaspoons grated lemon peel

1. Preheat the oven to 450°F. Line a 9-inch pie pan with the pastry.

2. In a large bowl, mix the sugar, flour, and cornmeal with a fork. Add the eggs, melted butter, milk, lemon juice, and grated lemon peel. Using a whisk or an electric mixer on low speed, mix until well blended. Pour into the pie shell.

3. Bake for 10 minutes. Lower the oven temperature to 350°F and bake 30 minutes longer or until the filling is golden and the tip of a sharp knife inserted in the center comes out clean. Serve warm or at room temperature.

Serves 8.

Chocolate Fudge Pie

For many of us, chocolate is the ultimate dessert, so it stands to reason that chocolate would be the perfect denouement for the ultimate in barbecue—no matter what style. Nothing tops off the taste of barbecue like chocolate.

1/2 recipe Homemade Pie Crust (page 157), unbaked, or a prepared crust

1/4 cup (1/2 stick) butter, melted and cooled

1 cup semisweet chocolate chips, melted and cooled

3/4 cup firmly packed brown sugar

3 eggs, lightly beaten

1 teaspoon vanilla

1/4 cup flour

1/4 teaspoon salt

Whipped cream or Homemade Vanilla Ice Cream (page 162), optional

1. Preheat the oven to 325°F. Line a 9-inch pie pan with the pastry.

2. In a small saucepan over low heat, melt the butter. Allow to cool completely.

3. Place the semisweet chocolate chips in a large microwave-safe bowl and heat on high power for 1 minute; stir. Repeat as necessary until the chocolate chips are melted. Allow to cool.

4. In a large bowl, combine the butter, brown sugar, eggs, vanilla, flour, and salt. Stir until the sugar is dissolved and the mixture is blended and smooth. Fold in the chocolate. Pour into the pie shell. Bake for 40 minutes or until the filling is set. Serve warm or at room temperature. Garnish with whipped cream or vanilla ice cream, if desired.

Serves 8.

Homemade Pie Crust

For those born with the knack, a pie crust seems simple. To the rest of us, it requires some practice. Just don't get anxious and overwork the dough. If things don't seem to be going well, return the dough to the refrigerator for 10 minutes or so.

I like to use stick shortening, which I've found makes a flakier, easier-to-work crust.

3 cups sifted flour	1¼ cups stick (or other) shortening
1 teaspoon salt	8 to 10 tablespoons cold water

1. Sift together the flour and salt. Using a pastry cutter, 2 knives, or your fingers, blend the shortening and flour until the mixture is crumbly. Stir in the cold water, adding just enough for the dough to hold together so you can form it into a smooth ball.

2. If using a food processor, combine the flour, salt, and shortening in the work bowl. Process on and off several times until the mixture is crumbly. With the motor running, add the water in a steady stream and process just until the mixture forms a ball.

3. Refrigerate the dough for 1 hour for easier handling. Divide the dough in half and roll out on a lightly floured board to make pastry for one 9-inch two-crust pie or two 9-inch single-crust pies. Roll the dough about 2 inches larger than the diameter of the pie pan. Drape the crust over the rolling pin and ease it into the pan, fitting it against the bottom and sides. The crust should overlap the edge of the pan by about ½ inch. Turn the crust under and shape the edge, using your fingers to create a fluted or pleated edge.

4. Fill and bake as directed in the pie recipe.

5. For a baked or "blind" crust, prick the bottom and sides of the dough with a fork. Place in a preheated 450°F oven for 10 minutes or just until the crust is set and begins to take on a golden cast. Cool before filling.

Makes enough dough for 1 double-crust pie or 2 single-crust pies.

Milk Chocolate Devil's Food Cake

If chocolate pie isn't intense enough to clear away the last vestiges of barbecue, this study in contrasting shades and flavors of chocolate ought to do it. Dark fudge layers get a generous smear of lighter milk chocolate frosting.

2 squares unsweetened chocolate	1 teaspoon vanilla
1½ cups sugar	¾ cup buttermilk
⅛ teaspoon salt	1 teaspoon baking soda
½ cup (1 stick) butter, softened at room temperature	1½ cups sifted flour
2 eggs, well beaten	Milk Chocolate Frosting (recipe follows)

1. Position a rack in the middle of the oven and preheat the oven to 375°F. Butter and flour two 9-inch square pans or two 9-inch round cake pans.

2. Place the chocolate in a 1-cup glass measure with ½ cup water. Microwave on high for 1 minute. Stir until the chocolate melts. Microwave on high for 20 seconds longer if needed to melt the chocolate. Stir until smooth and allow to cool.

3. In a large bowl, using an electric mixer on high speed, beat together the sugar, salt, and butter until the butter is light colored and fluffy, about 3 minutes. Beat in the eggs until the mixture is smooth and even colored.

4. On low speed, gradually add the cooled chocolate mixture, vanilla, buttermilk, and baking soda, beating until smooth. On low speed, add the flour in 3 equal parts. Beat well after each addition until batter is smooth. Pour the batter into the prepared cake pans.

5. Bake for 35 to 45 minutes or until a toothpick inserted in the center comes out clean. Remove from the oven and place on wire racks to cool.

6. Frost the top and sides of the layers with the frosting.

Serves 10 to 12.

SHORTCUT: *Grease and flour a 9 x 13-inch pan. Fill with the batter and bake for 40 to 45 minutes or until a toothpick inserted in the center comes out clean. Remove from the oven and place on a wire rack to cool. For layers, cut the cake crosswise in half; trim the layers until even. Or leave whole as a sheet cake.*

Milk Chocolate Frosting

This light frosting provides a nice color and flavor contrast to the deep darkness of devil's food layers.

½ cup (1 stick) butter	⅓ cup cocoa powder
⅓ cup milk	1 teaspoon vanilla
1 16-ounce package confectioners' sugar	

1. In a large microwave-safe glass mixing bowl with handle, combine the butter and milk. Microwave on high for 1 minute. Stir as needed to melt the butter. Or combine the butter and milk in a small saucepan and heat to boiling. Remove from the heat and stir to melt the butter.

2. Sift together the confectioners' sugar and cocoa. Using an electric mixer on high speed, gradually beat the sugar mixture into the butter and milk. Add the vanilla and beat until smooth.

3. Use to fill and frost a layer cake or frost the top of a sheet cake.

Makes 2 cups; enough for one 9-inch 2-layer cake or one 9 x 13-inch sheet cake.

Buttermilk Pound Cake

Pound cake is a staple dessert in many barbecue joints. Easy to make and delicious with or without a glaze, it makes a great everyday dessert. This is a large cake, more than enough for any but a large crowd. After baking and cooling, divide the cake. Wrap half tightly in foil and freeze so you'll have an emergency dessert.

1 cup (2 sticks) butter, softened at room temperature	½ teaspoon salt
1½ cups sugar	½ cup buttermilk or sour cream
4 eggs	1 teaspoon vanilla, lemon, or almond flavoring
2 cups flour	Lemon Glaze or Chocolate Glaze (recipes follow), optional
¾ teaspoon baking soda	

1. Position a rack in the middle of the oven and preheat the oven to 350°F. Butter and flour an angel food or Bundt cake pan or two 9 x 5-inch loaf pans.

2. In a large mixing bowl, using an electric mixer on high speed, whip the butter and sugar together until light and fluffy. Add the eggs, one at a time, beating well after each addition.

3. Sift together the flour, baking soda, and salt. Using a wooden spoon or the beater on low speed, add the flour mixture and buttermilk alternately in 2 parts to the butter mixture. Stir in the vanilla or other flavoring. Pour the batter into the prepared pan.

4. Bake for 45 to 50 minutes (35 to 40 minutes for loaf pans) or until a toothpick inserted in the center comes out clean. Cool for 5 minutes on a wire rack. Remove the cake from the pan. If using the lemon glaze, pour it over the cake while still warm. If using the chocolate glaze, allow the cake to cool completely, then pour it on.

Serves 12.

Lemon Glaze

Pour this simple glaze over warm pound cake. It's especially good with lemon-flavored pound cake.

½ cup confectioners' sugar	¼ cup lemon juice, preferably fresh, or as needed
1 teaspoon very finely grated lemon peel	

1. Stir together the confectioners' sugar, lemon peel, and lemon juice until smooth and just thin enough to drizzle and spread. Add more juice if needed.

2. Drizzle over warm pound cake, spreading to coat the top evenly. Let the glaze run down the sides of the cake.

Makes about ½ cup.

Chocolate Glaze

Rich and chocolatey, this glaze transforms a plain pound cake into a work of art. It's especially good with almond-flavored cake.

6 ounces semisweet chocolate, coarsely chopped or broken	¼ cup milk or heavy cream
¼ cup (½ stick) butter	

1. Combine the chocolate, butter, and milk in a microwave-safe mixing bowl with a handle. Microwave on high 30 seconds at a time, stirring at the end of each cooking time. Repeat until the chocolate is melted and the mixture is smooth. Or combine the ingredients in the top of a double boiler over simmering water. Heat and stir until the chocolate is melted and the mixture is smooth.

2. Let the glaze stand until slightly thickened but still pourable. Drizzle it over the top of cooled pound cake, letting it run down the sides.

Makes about 1 cup.

Homemade
Vanilla Ice Cream

Homemade ice cream is luscious by itself. It also adds dimension to most fruit desserts, especially pie or cobbler. Vanilla ice cream is the ultimate base for any perfectly fresh, lightly sweetened summer fruit.

2 cups hot milk	2 cups heavy cream, well chilled
1/2 cup sugar	1/4 teaspoon salt
4 egg yolks	1 tablespoon vanilla

1. In a medium saucepan, heat the milk over high heat until almost boiling. Remove from the heat and allow to cool slightly.

2. In a large saucepan, combine the sugar and egg yolks. Using an electric mixer, beat together until thickened. Stirring constantly or with the electric mixer on low speed, slowly pour the hot milk into the egg mixture. Add the milk slowly so the eggs don't cook.

3. Place the saucepan over low heat. Stir and cook until the custard is thick enough to coat the back of a spoon. Remove from the heat. If desired, pour through a strainer into a large pitcher or similar container. Cool slightly, then cover tightly and place in the refrigerator to cool completely.

4. Prepare an ice cream freezer according to the manufacturer's instructions. In the freezer container, combine the cooled custard, chilled heavy cream, salt, and vanilla. Freeze according to the manufacturer's instructions.

Serves 8.

Old-Fashioned Banana Pudding

The real deal, like Grandmother used to make . . . or like she made in your dreams.

1¼ cups sugar	1 teaspoon vanilla
3 tablespoons flour	Vanilla wafers
¼ teaspoon salt	4 ripe bananas, peeled and sliced
1½ cups milk	1 cup heavy cream, optional
3 eggs, separated	

1. In a medium saucepan, combine 1 cup of the sugar with the flour and salt, mixing well. Add the milk gradually, stirring constantly to mix well. Place over medium heat and cook until the mixture is thickened, stirring constantly. Remove from the heat and allow to cool slightly.

2. In a small bowl, beat the egg yolks until smooth and lemon colored. Stir a small amount of the hot milk mixture into the egg yolks, then stir the egg yolks into the hot milk. Stir in the vanilla. Remove from the heat and set aside.

3. Place the egg whites in a small mixer bowl. Beat on high speed with an electric mixer until foamy. While beating, gradually add the remaining ¼ cup sugar. Continue beating until stiff peaks form. Fold the egg whites into the pudding base.

4. Have ready a 1½-quart trifle dish or other deep dish with straight sides. Line the bottom of the dish with vanilla wafers. Top with a layer of pudding and a layer of bananas. Repeat with a second layer of vanilla wafers, pudding, and bananas. Top with a final layer of pudding.

5. Decorate with vanilla wafers around the edge of the bowl. Chill until serving time. Just before serving, whip the cream, if desired, and dollop on top of the pudding.

Serves 6 to 8.

Peach Cobbler

Peaches are a favorite from the Texas Hill Country to Atlanta. This two-crust cobbler shows off fresh summer peaches to best advantage.

8 cups peeled and sliced fresh peaches	3 tablespoons butter
2 cups plus 1 tablespoon sugar	1 recipe Homemade Pie Crust (page 157), unbaked, or a prepared crust
3 tablespoons all-purpose flour	
½ teaspoon ground nutmeg	2 tablespoons melted butter
½ teaspoon ground cinnamon	Homemade Vanilla Ice Cream (page 162) or your choice of packaged
2 tablespoons lemon juice	

1. Preheat the oven to 475°F. Spray a round 3-quart baking dish with cooking spray.

2. In a large saucepan, combine the peaches, 2 cups sugar, flour, nutmeg, and cinnamon and set over low heat. When the mixture bubbles, reduce the heat and simmer 10 minutes or until the peaches are tender. Remove from the heat and stir in the lemon juice and 3 tablespoons butter, stirring gently until the butter melts.

3. Spoon half of the peach filling into the baking dish. Top with a layer of pastry cut to fit the dish. Bake for 12 minutes or until golden brown. Remove from the oven and spoon the remaining peaches over the baked pastry. Top with a second layer of pastry cut to fit the dish. Pierce the top of the pastry with a fork to vent and brush with the melted butter. Sprinkle with 1 tablespoon sugar and bake for 10 to 15 minutes or until golden.

4. Remove from the oven and cool 10 minutes before serving. Place a warm scoop of cobbler in each dessert dish. Top with vanilla ice cream.

Serves 8 to 10.

Fried Fruit Pies

You know you're in the Deep South when you find a fresh hot fried pie. After all, Southerners have adapted virtually every dish to frying. Why not pies? A good fried pie is hard to come by these days; it's too labor intensive. Few places fry to order and instead fry them ahead, with soggy, greasy results. If you really want a good fried pie, you might have to make a batch yourself.

2 cups flour	1 egg, separated
1/2 teaspoon salt	1/3 cup vegetable shortening, melted
1/4 teaspoon sugar	1 16-ounce can peach or apple pie filling
1 teaspoon baking powder	Additional shortening or vegetable oil
3/4 cup heavy cream	for frying

1. In a medium bowl, combine the flour, salt, sugar, and baking powder. In a small bowl, mix together the cream, egg yolk, and melted shortening. Add the liquid ingredients to the flour mixture to make a soft dough. Cover and refrigerate about 2 hours.

2. Remove about half the dough from the refrigerator; keep the remainder chilled. Lightly flour a board. Pinch off a golf-ball-size piece of dough. Flatten the dough with your hands, then roll it into a thin round about the size of a saucer.

3. Place 2 tablespoons pie filling in the center of the dough. Fold over until the edges meet. Press the edges with a fork to seal. Repeat with the remaining dough to make about 1 dozen pies.

4. Beat the egg white until frothy, adding about 1 teaspoon water. Brush the edges of the pies with the egg white mixture to seal. Place the pies in the refrigerator and chill for 30 minutes to 1 hour.

5. In a large skillet, melt enough shortening or pour enough oil to reach a depth of about 2 inches. Heat to 375°F. Add the pies, no more than 2 or 3 at a time, and fry until golden. Turn once and cook until golden on the other side, about 3 to 5 minutes total. Drain well on absorbent paper.

6. Serve warm or at room temperature.

Makes 1 dozen.

sources

The following lists will be helpful in accessing the world of barbecue through associations, contests, classes, publications, sources of ingredients, and cooking equipment.

BARBECUE ASSOCIATIONS

International Barbecue Cookers Association (IBCA)
P.O. Box 300566, Arlington, TX 76007-0556
Phone: 817-548-8894
www.ibcabbq.org

Kansas City Barbecue Society (KCBS)
11514 Hickman Mills Dr., Kansas City, MO 64134
Phone: 800-963-5227 or 816-765-5891
Fax: 816-765-5860
www.bbqsearch.com
Email: KCBS@compuserve.com

Memphis in May (MIM)
245 Wagner Pl., Ste. 220, Memphis, TN 38103
Phone: 901-525-4611
www.memphisinmay.org

National Barbecue Association (NBBQA)
P.O. Box 9685, Kansas City, MO 64134-9865
Phone: 816-767-8311
Fax: 816-765-5860
www.bbq.about.com

North Carolina Pork Council (NCPC)
2300 Rexwoods Dr., Ste. 340, Raleigh, NC 27607
Phone: 919-781-0361
www.ncpork.org

BARBECUE CONTESTS

This list is by no means complete, but it does offer a geographic spread and includes some of the better-known events. As the calendar indicates, barbecue knows no season, but the big contests are clustered in October.

FEBRUARY

Houston Livestock Show and Rodeo World's Championship Bar-B-Que Contest
Contact: Tiffany Collins, P.O. Box 20070, Houston, TX 77225-0070
Phone: 713-791-9000
Fax: 713-794-9528
www.rodeohouston.com
E-mail: collins@rodeohouston.com

National Barbecue Association's Annual Meeting and Trade Show
(meeting locations vary)

Contact: Lee Henry, P.O. Box 9685,
Kansas City, MO 64134
Phone: 816-767-8311 or 888-909-2121
Fax: 816-765-5860
www.nbbqa.org
E-mail: nbbqa@nbbq.org

MARCH

Batesville Ozark Hawg BBQ Championship
Batesville, Arkansas
Contact: Lyndal Waits, 3396 Shade Tree
Dr., Batesville, AR 72501
Phone: 870-251-2374 or 870-698-2121
Fax: 870-251-2393
E-mail: lmwahpd@ipa.net

Beach, Blues & Barbecue
Flagler Beach, Florida
Contact: Jodie Bevel, P.O. Box 250, Flagler
Beach, FL 32136
Phone: 386-439-4882
Fax: 386-439-5881

Georgia Beef Barbecue Championship
Hawkinsville, Georgia
Contact: Linda Lane, Route 4, Box 12820,
Hawkinsville, GA 31036
Phone: 478-783-3458
www.shootthebull.org
E-mail: lrlane@cstel.net

APRIL

Fiesta Bowl Pigskin Classic BBQ
Tempe, Arizona
Contact: Mike Merucci, 120 S. Ashe Ave.,
Tempe, AZ 85281

Phone: 480-350-0900
Fax: 480-736-4165
www.tostitosfiestabowl.com
E-mail: mmerucci@fiestabowl.org

Tunica Rivergate Festival
Tunica, Mississippi
Contact: Brian Goff, P.O. Box 1888,
Tunica, MS 38676
Phone: 662-363-2865
Fax: 662-357-0378
www.rivergatefestival.com
E-mail: bgoff@watervalley.net

MAY

Arkansas State Championship
Delight, Arkansas
Contact: Mike Davis, P.O. Box 297,
Delight, AR 71940
Phone: 870-379-2774
Fax: 870-370-2932

Memphis in May
World Championship Barbecue Cooking
Contest
Contact: Floyd Benson, 245 Wagner
Place, Ste. 220, Memphis,
TN 38103
Phone: 901-525-4611
Fax: 901-525-4686
www.memphisinmay.org
E-mail: fbenson@memphisinmay.org

The Whistle Stop Festival and Rocket City
BBQ Cook-Off
Huntsville, Alabama
Phone: 800-678-1819

SOURCES
168

Fax: 256-564-8151

www.rocketcitybbq@earlyworks.com

E-mail: info@rocketcitybbq.com

Bar-B-Q and Blues Festival

Cushing, Oklahoma

Contact: Trisa A. Nicholas, 300 N. Harrison, Cushing, OK 74023

Phone: 918-225-3434

Fax: 918-225-3439

E-mail: cushingchamber.org

Great Lenexa Barbeque Battle

Lenexa, Kansas

Contact: Bill Nicks, 13420 Oak, Lenexa, KS 66215

Phone: 913-541-8592

Fax: 913-492-8118

www.ci.lenexa.ks.us

E-mail: bnicks@ci.lenexa.ks.us

The National Capital Barbecue Battle

Washington, D.C.

Contact: Doug and Kathy Halo (kshalo1@aol.com), 3809 Washington Woods Dr., Alexandria, VA 22309

Phone: 301-860-0630

Fax: 301-860-0639

www.bbq-usa.com

E-mail: barbecue1@aol.com

Official North Carolina State Barbecue Championship

Blue Ridge Barbecue Festival, 2753 Lynn Rd., Tryon, NC 28782

Phone: 828-859-RIBS (7427)

Iowa State Championship

Des Moines, Iowa

Contact: Anne Rehnstrom, 2320 Heatherwood Dr., W. Des Moines, IA 50265

Phone: 515-223-2622

Fax: 515-223-2646

www.iabbq.org

E-mail: anne.rehnstrom@porkboard.org

Best in the West Nugget Rib Cook-Off, Labor Day Weekend

Sparks, Nevada

Contact: Michele Malchow, John Ascuaga's Nugget, 1100 Nugget Ave., Sparks NV 89431

Phone: 775-356-3300 or 800-843-2427

www.januget.com

E-mail: mmalchow@janugget.com

American Royal Barbecue

Kansas City, Missouri

Contact: Tracy Satterfield, 1701 American Royal Court, Kansas City, MO 64102

Phone: 816-221-9800

Fax: 816-221-8189

www.americanroyal.com/bbq.htm

E-mail: amroyalbbq.aol.com

Barbecue Festival (not a cook-off but lots to eat)

Lexington, North Carolina

Contact: Kay Sing, P.O. Box 1642,
Lexington, NC 27293
Phone: 336-956-1880
Fax: 336-956-1647
www.barbecuefestival.com
E-mail: kay@barbecuefestival.com

Jack Daniel's World Championship Invitational Barbecue
Lynchburg, Tennessee
Contact: Tana Shupe, Jack Daniel's
Distillery, 3310 West End Ave.,
Nashville, TN 37203
Phone: 615-340-1000
www.jackdaniels.com
E-mail: tana_shupe@jackdaniels.com

North Carolina Championship Pork
Cook-Off
Raleigh, North Carolina
Contact: Beth Sawyers, NC Pork Council,
2300 Rexwoods Dr., Ste. 340, Raleigh,
NC 27607
Phone: 919-781-0361
www.ncpork.org
E-mail: market@ncpork.org

For more extensive lists of contests, try some
of these websites:

www.southernbarbecue.com
www.smokering.net
http://dmoz.org/Recreation/Food/Contests/
http://www.bbqjudge.com/
www.barbecue.com (contests)
www.bbqsearch.com (contests)
*www.southfest.com (festivals
nc/sc/fl/a/va/tn)*

The following publish information about
contests:

Kansas City Bull Sheet
Kansas City BBQ Society
Contact: Carolyn Wells, 11514 Hickman
Mills Dr., Kansas City, MO 64134
Phone: 800-963-5227
Fax: 816-765-5860
E-mail: kcbs@compuserve.com

National Barbecue News
Contact: Joe Pelts, P.O. Box 981, Douglas,
GA 31533
Phone: 800-385-0002 or 912-384-0001
www.barbecuenews.com
E-mail: Joe@barbecuenews.com
1-year subscription, $20; 2 years, $36;
3 years, $52

CLASSES ON BARBECUE

Classes are available for would-be barbecue judges as well as competitive cooks.

CLASSES ON JUDGING BARBECUE

Kansas City Barbecue Society
Contact: Carolyn Wells, Executive Director, 11514 Hickman Mills Dr., Kansas
City, MO 64134
Phone: 800-963-KCBS (5227)
E-mail: kcbs@compuserve.com

Memphis in May Judging School
Memphis in May World Championship
Barbecue Cooking Contest

Contact: Pam Hetzel, 245 Wagner Pl.,
    Ste. 220, Memphis, TN 38103
Phone: 901-525-4611, ext. 118
Fax: 901-525-4686
www.memphisinmay.org
E-mail: phetsel@memphisinmay.org

CLASSES ON COOKING BARBECUE COMPETITIVELY

CIA of Smoke Cooking Mail Order
    Course
1342 Columbine, Denver, CO 80205-2304
Phone: 303-321-7424
www.bbqcookingschool.com
E-mail: BBQcookingschool@uswest.net

Kansas City Barbecue Society
Instructors: Paul Kirk, Ed Roith,
    Smoky Hale, Jerry Roach, Lew (Doc)
    Miller
11514 Hickman Hills Dr., Kansas City, MO
    64134
Phone: 800-963-KCBS (5227) or
    816-765-5891
Fax: 816-765-5860
www.bbqsearch.com
E-mail: KCBS@compuserve.com

New England Barbecue Society Cooking
    School
Contact: Charlie Pini, 161 S. Main St.
    Middleton, MA 09149
Phone: 913-262-6029
www.nebs.org
E-mail: burndtends@carlotta.com

INSTRUCTORS

Smoky Hale
8168 Hwy. 98 East, McComb, MS 39648
Phone: 601-684-0001
Fax: 601-684-0052
www.barbecuen.com
E-mail: cchale@telpak.net

Paul Kirk, seven-time world champion,
    offers classes around the country.
Phone: 913-262-6029
www.bbqcookoff.com/school.htm
E-mail: bbqbaron@hotmail.com

Lew (Doc) Miller
14 South 2nd Ave., Marshalltown, IO 50158
Phone: 515-753-6640
E-mail: lewmiller1@prodigy.net

Jerry Roach
J.R. Enterprises School of Southern
    Cooking, Route 1, Box 249A, Dewitt,
    AR 72042
Phone: 501-946-2780 or 800-432-8187
E-mail: jr@jrenterprises.com

Ed Roith
P.O. Box 86004, Shawnee Mission, KS
    66286-0004
Phone: 913-422-4730

BARBECUE PUBLICATIONS

In addition to information about contests and festivals (including results), these publications are full of tips, recipes, and product information.

Goat Gap Gazette
Chili and barbecue monthly newsletter;
     $18/year
Contact: P.O. Box 800, Brookesmith, TX
     76827-0800
Phone: 915-646-6914

National Barbecue News
Monthly publication with cook-off
     calendar, recipes; $18/year
Contact: Joe Phelps or Don Gillis,
     P.O. Box 981, Douglas, GA 31533
Phone: 912-384-0001 or
     800-385-0002
Fax: 912-384-4220
E-mail: joedoc@almatel.net

The Pits
Monthly newsletter of the IBCA;
     $18/year
Contact: Susan Tindall, 7714 Hillard,
     Dallas, TX 75217
Phone: 214-398-4374

SOURCES OF INGREDIENTS

These purveyors are recommended by some of the experts I've met and whose products I've used while researching this book. Phone, fax, or e-mail for catalogs or information. Also see the lists of restaurants in the regional chapters. Many sell their seasonings and sauces.

SEASONINGS

Ingredients Corporation of America
Full line of spices, plus custom spice
     blending
Mailing address: 676 Huron Ave.,
     Memphis, TN 38107
Phone: 901-525-4422
Fax: 901-525-4425

Mo Hotta Mo Betta
Full line of spices and sauces
Mailing address: P. O. Box 4136, San Luis
     Obispo, CA 93403
Phone: 800-462-3220
Fax: 800-618-4454

Obie-Cue's Texas Spice
Prize-winning dry rub blends for all styles
     of barbecue
Mailing address: P.O. Box 951, Lancaster,
     TX 75146-7951
Phone: 972-641-2660
Fax: 972-227-0686
www.obiecue.com
E-mail: Obiecue@flash.net

Pendery's
Barbecue and chili spices
Mailing address: 1221 Manufacturing, Dallas, TX 75207
Phone: 800-533-1870
Fax: 214-761-1966

Tabby's Inc.
North Carolina blends from barbecue
    judge Jim "Trim" Tabb
Mailing address: P.O. Box 99, Tryon, NC
    28782
Phone: 828-859-5976
Fax: 828-859-9918
www.tabbys.com
E-mail: tabbys@aol.com

Vann's Spices
Full line of spices and blends, plus custom
    spice blending
Mailing address: 6105 Oakleaf Ave..
    Baltimore, MD 21201
Phone: 410-358-3007 or
    800-367-4709
www.earthy.com

Also see these websites:

www.cookperfect.com
www.bbqsource.com

BARBECUE SAUCES

Finding a barbecue sauce is about as tough
as finding fat on a hog. Sheer numbers of
available sauces make deciding which sauce
to choose daunting. Here are some sources
that represent a variety of regional styles or a
specific style.

El Paso Chile Company
Texas-style and gourmet sauces
Mailing address: 909 Texas Ave., El Paso,
    TX 79901
Phone: 888-4-SALSAS

www.elpasochile.com
E-mail: hola@elpasochile.com

George's Hot Barbecue Sauce, Piedmont
    Style
Mailing address: 1173 Womble Rd.,
    Nashville, NC 27856
Phone: 252-459-3084
Fax: 252-459-3505
E-mail: n2sauce@aol.com

Maurice's Gourmet Barbeque
The most famous South Carolina mustard
    barbecue sauce
Mailing address: P.O. Box 6847, West
    Columbia, SC 29171
Phone: 800-MAURICE
www.mauricesbbq.com
E-mail: mail@mauricesbbq.com

Also see these websites:

www.americabestbbq.com
www.cookperfect.com
www.4bbq.com

SOURCES OF EQUIPMENT

Many manufacturers make gas-fired
grills, as well as cookers that use
wood and/or charcoal. These are some of
the best-known names. Phone, fax, or e-mail
for catalogs or information.

Bar-B-Que Pits by Klose
Mailing address: 2214½ W. 34th St., Hous-
    ton. TX 77018

Phone: 800-487-7487
Fax: 713-686-8793

The Brinkmann Corp.
Mailing address: 4215 McEwen Rd.,
    Dallas, TX 75244
Phone: 800-468-5252

Hasty-Bake
Mailing address: P.O. Box 471285, Tulsa,
    OK 74147-1285
Phone: 916-665-8220 or 800-426-6836
Fax: 918-665-8225
www.hastybake.com
E-mail: ahicks@gorilla.net

New Braunfels Smoker Co.
Mailing address: P.O. Box 310698, New
    Braunfels, TX 78130
Phone: 800-232-3398
Fax: 210-629-9140

Patio Classic Grills (formerly Kingsford
    Charcoal Grills)
Sold under Martha Stewart label at KMart
www.patioclassics.com
E-mail: sbertloff@porcelainmetals.com

Weber-Stephen Products
Mailing address: 250 S. Hicks Rd.,
    Palatine, IL 60067
Phone: 800-446-1071

Also see these websites:

www.cooking.com
www.ourhouse.com

ON-LINE SOURCES

BARBECUE'N ON THE INTERNET

A comprehensive page with information on contests, equipment, and techniques. Includes information from expert Smoky Hale. www.barbecuen.com

BBQSEARCH.COM

A comprehensive page with links to the barbecue world. Self-described "portal" to the barbecue world. Recipes, equipment, forum, information on sauces and wood, and more. www.bbqsearch.com

PIG OUT PUBLICATIONS

The only company devoted exclusively to publishing barbecue and grill cookbooks. The website provides an on-line catalog, as well as links to other BBQ websites. www.pigoutpublications.com

THE SMOKE RING

A comprehensive web index of barbecue-related web pages. It is a continuous loop of websites with icons that take you from one site to the next. Information on equipment, seasonings, cookers, and more. www.smokering.net

glossary

Speaking the language and understanding the jargon are important in any endeavor, including barbecue.

Barbecue grill: An appliance for cooking meat over wood coals, charcoal, gas, or electricity at sustained low temperatures. *See* Grill.

Barbecue pit: A hole in the ground for containing wood coals over which a grate or rack to hold the meat is placed for barbecuing. Also, a brick or masonry construction for containing coals over which meat is cooked on a rack. A portable large metal construction for the same purpose.

Bark: Burnt ends.

Barrel smoker: A kind of barbecue cooker that is made from a barrel or is shaped like a barrel, often with a firebox attached at one end to hold the coals for indirect heat.

Baste, basting sauce: A thin, usually acidic sauce brushed on meat during cooking to tenderize and flavor it. Also called a mop.

Brisket: The large, flat, fat-covered cut of beef that distinguishes Texas barbecue.

Brown: North Carolina term for the brown crispy trimmings or end slices of barbecued pork.

Brunswick stew: A rich stew served with barbecue in North Carolina.

Burgoo: A rich stew served with barbecue in Tennessee and Kentucky.

Burnt ends, Bark: Kansas City term for charred trimmings from a brisket.

Charcoal: A fuel used to fire barbecue. Charcoal is the remains of wood burned in an oxygen-deprived atmosphere to prevent flaming. Lighter and less bulky than hardwood, it is a convenient fuel and doesn't take as long to burn down as wood. May be supplemented with soaked wood chips or with hardwood for flavoring the smoke. Despite the convenience of charcoal, hardwood is the preferred fuel for traditional barbecue, although even experienced pit masters often use some charcoal.

Cooker: A barbecue grill or barbecue pit.

Dip: *See* Sauce.

Direct heat: A heat source that is directly under the meat.

Dry ribs: Ribs that are not sauced during cooking.

Dry rub: *See* Rub.

Firebox: A container that holds the fuel for indirect heat in a barbecue cooker. Usually attached to the end of a cooker.

Grate: *See* Grill.

Grill (n): 1. A rack on which food is placed for cooking over a heat source. Also called a grate.

2. An appliance with a rack that most commonly uses coals (or another heat source, such as gas) for cooking. *(v):* 1. To cook over high temperatures and direct heat.

Hardwood: The type of densely structured, slow-burning wood preferred for cooking and flavoring barbecue. Hickory, oak, and mesquite are some of the more popular.

Hushpuppies: Cylinders or balls of fried cornmeal dough. Eaten with Carolina barbecue.

Indirect heat: A heat source that is to the side or away from the meat, often in a separate firebox.

Kettle grill: A round cooker with a single grate. Small and easy to store but better for grilling than for barbecuing.

Mop: *See* Baste.

Picnic: Lower part of the front shoulder of a pig; used for pulled pork.

Pit: *See* Barbecue pit.

Pork butt or Boston butt: Upper part of the front shoulder of a pig; used for pulled pork.

Pork shoulder: Entire front leg and shoulder of a hog; usually divided into two cuts, the Boston butt and the picnic.

Red slaw: Style of slaw associated with barbecue in the Piedmont (western part) of North Carolina.

Ribs: Refers to pork ribs unless otherwise specified, as in beef ribs.

Rub: A blend of dry spices used to coat meat before it is barbecued. It should be patted or rubbed into the surface of the meat so it adheres; hence, the term.

Sauce: Refers to the sauce used on barbecue after cooking (sometimes added in the final cooking period to glaze the meat, particularly ribs); also called dip. A sauce is different from the high-acid mops used for basting.

Skinning ribs: Removing the tough membrane from the bony side of ribs for better absorption of seasoning and sauce and for easier eating.

Smoker: A cooker that uses indirect or very low heat to cook meat and season it with smoke.

Snouts: Pronounced "snoots." Barbecued pig faces, considered a delicacy in St. Louis, where they are an art form.

Water smoker: A light metal appliance with a bottom rack for fuel, wood, or charcoal and a top rack for meat. An open pan of water or another liquid is positioned between the racks. Smokers make it almost impossible to dry out the meat from overcooking, but the moist heat from the liquid doesn't produce the same texture as pit barbecuing or barbecuing over indirect heat.

Wet ribs: Ribs that are heavily sauced during cooking. They are moist, sticky, and messy to eat.

Whole hog: A barbecued whole pig.

bibliography

Butler, Cleora. *Cleora's Kitchen: The Memoir of a Cook & Eight Decades of Great American Food.* Tulsa, Okla.: Council Oaks Books, 1985.

Davis, Ardie. *The Great Barbecue Sauce Book.* Berkeley, Calif.: Ten Speed Press, 1999.

Edge, John T. *A Gracious Plenty: Recipes and Recollections from the American South.* New York: G. P. Putnam's Sons, 1998.

Elie, Lois Eric. *Smokestack Lightning: Adventures in the Heart of Barbecue Country.* New York: Farrar, Straus & Giroux, 1996.

Garner, Bob. *North Carolina Barbecue: Flavored by Time.* Winston-Salem, N.C.: John F. Blair, 1996.

Hale, C. Clark "Smoky." *The Great American Barbecue & Grilling Manual.* McComb, Miss.: Abacus Publishing Company, 1999.

Jamison, Cheryl Alters, and Bill Jamison. *Born to Grill.* Boston: Harvard Common Press, 1998.

———. *Smoke & Spice.* Boston: Harvard Common Press, 1994.

Kansas City Barbecue Society. *The Kansas City Barbecue Society Cookbook.* Kansas City: Kansas City Barbecue Society, 1998,

Kirk, Paul. *Paul Kirk's Championship Barbecue Sauces.* Boston: Harvard Common Press, 1998.

Martinez, Matt Jr., and Steve Pate. *Matt Martinez's Culinary Frontier: A Real Texas Cookbook.* New York: Doubleday, 1997.

Raichlen, Steven. *The Barbecue! Bible.* New York: Workman Publishing, 1998.

Sohn, Mark F. *Mountain Country Cooking: A Gathering of the Best Recipes from the Smokies to the Blue Ridge.* New York: St. Martin's Press, 1996.

St. Laurent, Jonathan, and Charles Neave. *Uncle Billy's Downeast Barbecue Book.* West Rockport, Maine: Dancing Bear Books, 1991.

Voltz, Jeanne. *Barbecued Ribs and Other Great Feeds.* New York: Knopf, 1985.

LIQUID AND DRY MEASURE EQUIVALENCIES

CUSTOMARY	METRIC
¼ teaspoon	1.25 milliliters
½ teaspoon	2.5 milliliters
1 teaspoon	5 milliliters
1 tablespoon	15 milliliters
1 fluid ounce	30 milliliters
¼ cup	60 milliliters
⅓ cup	80 milliliters
½ cup	120 milliliters
1 cup	240 milliliters
1 pint *(2 cups)*	480 milliliters
1 quart *(4 cups, 32 ounces)*	960 milliliters *(.96 liter)*
1 gallon *(4 quarts)*	3.84 liters
1 ounce *(by weight)*	28 grams
¼ pound *(4 ounces)*	114 grams
1 pound *(16 ounces)*	454 grams
2.2 pounds	1 kilogram *(1,000 grams)*

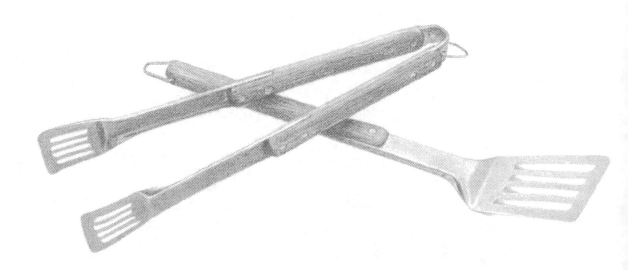

index